HOW TO
Claim Your
POWER

"In a small, power-packed volume, Dr. Helm addresses the most formidable task in recovery from childhood victimization: reclaiming personal power as an adult."

Laura Walker Kerzner, M.S.
Marriage and Family Therapist

"The concept of power seems to be a dirty word among those who have been the victims of the abuse of power such as sexual abuse victims . . . It was refreshing to see it addressed directly."

Anna Sabin, MSW
Rape Crisis Center, Ogden, Utah

"'Survivors' are encouraged to become 'thrivers' in this important book by Gretchen Helm. Empowerment is the center of what it means to be human."

Rev. Dr. M. B. Handspicker
Professor, Andover Newton Theological School

"*How to Claim Your Power* guides and structures sound therapeutic intervention . . . A must reading for victim and therapist alike."

Dr. James R. Sorensen
Licensed Psychologist

"Gretchen Helm's book reads with a passionate intensity that reflects [the author's] commitment to help others speak the truth of their lives that may set them free and help them claim their power."

Brita Gill-Austern, Ph.D.
Assistant Professor of Pastoral Care and Practical Theology
Andover Newton Theological School

"*How to Claim Your Power* is a book full of the power of example and especially useful to help therapists better appreciate the special needs of female survivors."

Lawrence Kistler, Ph.D.
Director of Counseling, Interfaith Counseling Service, Inc.

HOW TO
Claim Your
POWER

The Critical Step Beyond Survival

GIBBS·SMITH
→P
PUBLISHER

SALT LAKE CITY

Dr. Gretchen Helm

First edition
95 94 93   6 5 4 3 2 1

This is a Peregrine Smith Book, published by
Gibbs Smith, Publisher
P.O. Box 667
Layton, UT 84041

Cover design by Mary Ellen Thompson
Interior design by K. C. Muscolino

Manufactured in the United States of America

Library of Congress Cataloging-in-Publication Data

Helm, Gretchen
How to claim your power ; the critical step beyond survival / Gretchen
Helm.
p. cm.
ISBN 0-87905-482-4
1. Adult child sexual abuse victims—United States—Psychology.
2. Women—United States—Psychology. I. Title.
HV6570.2.H45 1993
362.7'6—dc20   92-14550
CIP

To Norm, who taught me the power of love.

Contents

Acknowledgments

I am deeply grateful to all the women who shared their stories and their lives with me, allowing me to join them in their struggle to heal from the wounds of childhood sexual abuse. Their courage has been an inspiration to me and now will inspire other women to keep moving forward in their recovery.

The survivors in this book wanted their stories to be told. They wanted their voices to finally be heard so the cycle of sexual abuse of children could be broken. I tried to tell the truth of their lives as honestly as I could and hope that I succeeded.

As victims of childhood sexual abuse, we were joined together in our pain. As survivors we can now be joined together in claiming our power. Finally.

Dr. Gretchen Helm
Albuquerque, New Mexico
February 1993

She's a sparrow when she's broken
but she's an eagle when she flies.

—Dolly Parton

Introduction

Women who were sexually abused as children are coming forward in great numbers to tell the world of the pain and trauma they suffered as victims. They speak of the terrible consequences they have had to endure—drug abuse, suicide attempts, inability to form intimate relationships, difficulty with trust, and psychiatric hospitalizations, to list just a few.

It's important that we hear these stories and become aware of the tragic effects of sexual abuse. The playwright Ibsen said that we must speak of evil or it will grow like mushrooms in the basement. The light of truth has finally been focused upon one of the most devastating and destructive things a young child can experience, and many women are now able to begin the process of healing their wounded and broken spirits.

However, it's just as important for us to learn about women who have survived the pain of their earlier abuse and who serve as beacons to others who are struggling to heal from their own wounds. Many women have been joined together as victims. They share the pain of having been violated and hurt as children. As victims they were isolated and alienated, afraid and confused. When they finally found the courage to speak of their victimization, they learned that they belonged to a sisterhood of survivors who knew, as they did, what it meant to be victims of childhood sexual abuse. It's time now for women to share the experiences of their recovery and the sources of their strength and power to help other survivors know what possibilities exist for them.

Women who have spoken of their abuse and sought help in dealing with its effects are now finding ways to go forward as strong, resourceful, and powerful people. They are not content with merely surviving; they want and need to feel in control of their lives, to make choices that are theirs, to say "yes" when they mean "yes" and "no" when they mean "no." Women who were sexually abused as children need to learn, sometimes for the first time, that they can be powerful and channel that power in appropriate and productive ways.

Healing is a process. It begins with admitting that something happened that was hurtful and wrong. There are resources, some of which are noted in this book, that help a survivor through this first phase when she confronts the reality of her abuse and begins the process of healing. The next step in the process is therapy that helps a survivor build a much-needed trust relationship and share her experiences and their effect upon her life. Some women then join with other survivors in a group process that reinforces and validates their recovery. Some women join movements that provide a means for them to eradicate the causes of child sexual abuse in society and in this way protect children from the trauma of sexual victimization.

I have counseled many women who want to claim the power that was denied them as victims and to become all that they were meant to be. They are searching for ways to accomplish this and look to other survivors who have gone beyond their pain and are examples of the power of the human spirit to transcend and renew. This book provides adult survivors with examples of how power can be used effectively and shows how some women have found the source of their own power and learned to use it appropriately and well. This book also shows how the power that once was used to victimize can be redirected by adult survivors to enhance their lives and avoid further victimization.

This book is about healing and hope. Anyone who has been a victim of childhood sexual abuse, as well as therapists, family and friends of victims, clergy, and community workers will be interested in knowing more about how to claim the power that was denied to victims.

How to Claim Your Power is a book that is intended for survivors who have found some benefit in therapy, who are aware of the pitfalls of victimization and who want to increase their power and also control their lives. If a survivor is just beginning to deal with her abusive past, this book can be seen as the light at the end of the tunnel—a promise of what a survivor can do and where she can be with time and healing. The sequence of the book is presented in much the same way healing progresses for most survivors. It begins with admitting that the problem of sexual abuse is a reality in one's life. The next step is dealing with the consequences of the abuse, which includes healing. At this point in the book, information is offered to therapists and to survivors to assist in the healing process. The final phase is to build upon the strengths and increase the power a survivor has discovered within herself. At this point the book presents examples of survivors who have claimed their power and can offer encouragement and hope to survivors who are ready to take this critical step beyond survival. The book concludes with concrete suggestions to help survivors maintain their power and continue growing ever more powerful.

This book can be used as a resource at any point as a woman evolves from victim to survivor. It can be used as a self-help manual if therapy is not available, or it can be used in conjunction with therapy. However, *How to Claim Your Power* is most useful in the final stages of healing, when a survivor is acutely aware of the consequences of her abuse and has experienced some healing already. This book helps the survivor to claim the power she has discovered within herself and to learn ways in which she can strengthen and maintain that power. I ask you to read this book in that spirit.

The Steps to Power

At the end of each chapter is a brief questionnaire that will help you learn more about how power plays out in your life. As you read the material, certain thoughts and ideas will come to you. Take the time to include these insights on the questionnaires so you can chart your personal evolution from victimization to power. If you are in therapy, or intend to be, you may find that these questionnaires can be helpful in providing important information to your therapist. The steps begin with learning about where the power is in your life, where you may have become stuck as a victim, and what the consequences are of your abuse. Before you go forward as a powerful survivor, you are then asked to note those women whom you know to have been victims but who have gone on to live powerful, productive lives. The next step is to find your power and to identify those areas in which you are strong and resourceful so that you can build upon these strengths.

A way in which to reinforce your power is to internalize powerful, positive messages on a regular and consistent basis. The next step asks you to do just that. As you replace the negative, self-defeating beliefs about yourself that so many survivors still carry with them, you will find that you are building a new and different base on which to build your powerful life.

The final steps challenge you to CLAIM your power, CHOOSE your power, and USE your power. Once you have completed these steps, you will find a new way to approach situations in your life that will lead to greater success and happiness. You may even want to answer the questionnaires again, after a period of time has elapsed, to learn how you have progressed in the process of claiming and using your personal power.

Keep in mind that there are numerous ways in which power is expressed. Some women are visibly powerful. They are bold and dramatic in the ways they use their power. It is clear to all who come in contact with them that these overtly powerful women are strong and resourceful. Then there are women who are more subtle in their use of power and whose personal styles tend towards the less flamboyant and more subdued expression of power. There is no one style that is right for all women. The important thing is that each woman feels confident and strong, capable of setting boundaries and limits, able to make her own decisions and choices; a woman who is not a victim but a powerful survivor who is in control of her life.

These steps should help you to gain more insight about yourself as you continue to channel the considerable strength you developed as a victim. This strength, when transformed into power, will be a force for enhancing your life and realizing your full potential; it will help you to do so much more than merely surviving the trauma of childhood sexual abuse.

Sexual abuse survivors have much to tell us about pain and suffering. We need to hear them and support their courageous efforts to heal from their victimization. Survivors are also telling of their victories, their triumph over the tragedy of childhood abuse, and we need to listen to these stories as well. They are sources of inspiration and hope to anyone who has ever felt powerless to change her life for the better. We need to hold the broken sparrow in loving and safe hands and grieve the pain of her brokenness and loss. We also need to rejoice and celebrate with grateful, wondering hearts the eagle as she flies.

The Next Step

While survivors may come from varied cultures and ethnic backgrounds, the misuse of power and the violation of trust affects all people in much the same way. Pain, disappointment, anger and healing transcend cultural mores and norms. However, the culture in which a woman lives, loves, and works may view her power in very different ways. That is a complex issue that touches upon anthropological and sociological factors requiring far more attention than can be given in this book. Perhaps another writer will be inspired to go yet one more step and help us understand how survivors who have claimed their power affect and are affected by their culture.

I invite you, the reader, whatever your interest or concern about adult survivors of childhood sexual abuse, to join with me in taking the next step of claiming your power. If, after having read this book, you know of other necessary and important stages for us to take in this journey of healing, then by all means provide yet another step. Find the power within yourself to add your piece, your voice, your part of the building process. This step is yours to build on.

Power and the Sexually Abused Child

1

*In the same way one can say that
cannibalism is not simply about eating,
incest is not simply about sex.*
— *Nachmani*

Sexual abuse is always an issue of power. It's not about affection or caring; it is not done in the name of educating a child. It's about power. Children have no power. They can't vote or hold public office or otherwise enjoy the privileges of adulthood. They are virtually powerless, at least in the ways we have come to understand power. Children are vulnerable and fragile creatures who must depend upon those who are more powerful to meet their needs.

Now put the child into a relationship with an adult, particularly an adult caretaker. The situation becomes one in which the child, who is powerless, must rely upon the adult for all that is necessary to sustain life and foster growth so that the child develops into a reasonably healthy individual. There is usually, by virtue of the closeness of the relationship and the bonds of family which exist, a trust that develops in the child. Introduce into this an element of sexual behavior initiated by the adult, and you clearly have the misuse of power. The child is powerless to stop or escape from this behavior or, in the case of a very young, socially isolated child, may not even know that it's wrong. The situation may feel wrong or bad, but lots of things do, and the child is expected to accept whatever the adult says is okay.

When sexual abuse occurs and the child has no means by which to escape, the child learns a profound lesson. The message is: "You have no choice about this, and you have no power. You are my victim." From that point on, the child expects that external events or circumstances will not be within her control. She is at the mercy of whatever or whomever makes choices that affect her. While the consequences of sexual abuse for a male victim differ in some ways from those for a female victim, it should be noted at this point that whether a victim is male or female, he or she learns a very painful lesson about being powerless over the abuse.

It's important for this to be agreed upon at the outset. The premise of this book is that those of us who were sexually abused as children have not just had our power taken from us through our victimization, but we indeed have never learned how to adequately develop our personal power and tap into it throughout our lives. For many of us, the families from which we were supposed to learn the skills for successful living were ill equipped to teach us what they did not know themselves. Some families merely repeat the cycle of victimization that they were part of as children. They are unable to teach their children the appropriate use of power because they never learned it themselves. It's time to break that cycle so that adults can properly teach their children how to be strong and powerful because they have learned how to be appropriately powerful themselves.

This is how it's supposed to happen: The adults within the family or those people who are entrusted to care for us have the responsibility to teach us how to live life and live it well. They are the ones with the power and the responsibility to do this job. It doesn't matter whether or not the majority of families have what it takes to nurture and guide their children to adulthood. What we're talking about is what's *supposed* to happen.

As young children, we begin to test the limits of our power. That process begins as an automatic response to the discomfort of being in a wet diaper or alone in a room without the comfort of a loving face looking down on us. Our cries seem to bring relief for our situation, and we learn that we have the power to affect our world and the people who inhabit it. Because we tend to repeat those things that meet with some amount of success, we try new and creative ways to get what we want and what we need (or think we need). Our sense of personal power is beginning to develop, and we're off! About the time we're in our second year, we really start to test the limits, thus the phrase "terrible twos." Everything is proceeding according to plan. In order to deal successfully with the world for whatever time is allotted to us from the cradle to the grave, we need power, and power requires a lot of time to be refined and internalized. So the child who balks or refuses or resists is merely "trying out" and "trying on" the cloak of power.

The job of the caretaker, then, is to help frame and channel the power of the child so that it becomes a positive source of energy for this developing person. A great deal of this is done by the caretaker setting reasonable and safe limits within which the child can complete this important phase of his or her development. Probably the most effective way caretakers accomplish this task of teaching the child how to find and use power is by example. It's usually referred to as "modeling," but setting an example says it just as well.

If the child observes the parents using their power in effective, just, and responsible ways, then the child learns an important lesson. Children are, after all, blank slates on which their parents and caretakers write their first lessons.

This is what is supposed to happen, but in families that are dysfunctional or unhealthy or otherwise incapable of responsible parenting, children grow up without learning how to appropriately use their power. Instead they are fueled by the energy of pain or sadness or rage. That's where a lot of us who were sexually abused as children end up. We get stuck in these cycles of debilitating feelings and can never go forward. The first step a survivor makes in beginning the process from powerlessness to claiming her power is to acknowledge the abuse of her past and talk about her experiences as a victim.

Many sexual abuse survivors have broken the silence about their victimization. They have told about the terrible consequences of having been victimized as vulnerable, impressionable children. The toll that sexual victimization has taken in the lives of survivors is immeasurable. The suffering has been, and continues to be, terrible and tragic. For many people it's time to move beyond the limbo state of pain and dysfunction and to gain the power that is important for everyone to have in order to function in the best possible way.

There are a number of problems and dynamics shared by women who were sexually abused as children. Before adult survivors can claim their power, these issues must be identified and explored. It's important to begin first with where you have been, and may still be, before beginning to move onward. Many of the problems discussed in this chapter apply to women who were sexually abused within the context of their families. However, survivors of abuse outside the family, including victims of acquaintance or date rape, share many of the same experiences and feelings as incest victims and must go through the same recovery process.

Abuse within the family and abuse outside the family have both similar and different effects on individuals, and these will be pointed out as they are discussed. As this book evolves, however, the reader will begin to see that victims of physical, emotional, and sexual abuse share a great deal. In fact some of the stories used as illustrations involve women who did not suffer childhood sexual abuse but have been abused in other ways. In this way women who have suffered from any type of victimization can see their lives reflected in the experiences of their sisters and be assured that victory is possible by viewing the lives of many who have successfully turned tragedy into triumph.

Issues for Women
Sexually Abused Within Their Families

Intimacy

Intimacy is difficult for a victim of sexual abuse to achieve. The memories of the abuse, the fear of losing control, the anger at having been violated are all triggered during intimacy, even with a loved one in a consenting relationship. For many partners of sexual abuse victims, this is difficult to understand and to cope with. It is hard for them to accept that they are not responsible for their partner's pain—only the catalyst for the painful and unpleasant memories.

Sexual abuse victims react differently to their abuse. Some victims, continually reinforced and validated for their bodies, learn to use their bodies to continue feeling that they are worth something. Oftentimes this becomes the only way in which they can feel affirmed. This explains, in part, why promiscuity and prostitution are major consequences of childhood sexual abuse.

For other victims, intimacy is so abhorrent to them that they refrain from being involved in any relationships that require intimate behavior. They maintain a distance that feels safe and nonthreatening, a distance that does not evoke the memories of their childhood abuse.

Still, for many sexual abuse victims, their need to be connected with another and to have someone they can depend upon finally, leads them to choose the most socially acceptable means of forming this connection—marriage. However, the intimacy of this relationship stirs up many painful feelings and also leads once more to a reliance upon dissociation. Again, the sexual abuse victim finds herself isolated, feeling guilty, unable to say "no," and protecting her partner from knowledge of her past and the reality of her pain.

Choice

Children who are sexually abused do not have a choice. Their ability to choose is taken from them the moment they are violated by a trusted person in their lives. They learn how to be victims—victims who accept their abuse because they have no options; victims who are powerless and without resources. They grow up believing that it will never be any different for them, that they will always be unable to make choices in their lives. They hold onto the image of powerlessness and continue, oftentimes, to let other people determine their fate. When victims continue to LET things happen rather than MAKE things happen, they reinforce their feelings of not being in control, not being able to make choices for themselves. And the cycle continues.

Telling the Secret

Sexual abuse survivors keep the secret of their abuse oftentimes for many years and sometimes forever. There are many reasons why victims cannot or will not share the fact that they were sexually abused, and these reasons are complex. Consider the fact that a young, trusting, dependent and socially isolated child is getting a number of things that she needs—that all children need—as a result of the abuse. She receives affection, attention, affirmation, and a sense that she is somehow taking care of this person that she knows is deficient on some level. That gives her a feeling of being necessary and worthwhile and, at the same time, causes her to feel guilty and bad about the sexual abuse. The victim has confused, ambivalent feelings. She may feel unsafe and threatened; she may also feel that she has tremendous power and control, although this power and control is inappropriate and ineffective. Sexual-abuse victims learn the misuse of power and also form a warped view of the world. Their isolation and disconnectedness from the outside world maintains for the victim a sense of being alone and without resources, which is a reality. This, above all, encourages a victim to keep the secret.

However, by not sharing the fact that they were violated by a trusted and loved person in their lives at a time when they were vulnerable and impressionable, victims form a number of beliefs which can affect them for the rest of their lives. Until victims of sexual abuse are helped to dispel the myth that they were responsible for the abuse, that they will betray the abuser and their families if they tell what happened, that they are bad and therefore not worthy of help, the secret will remain buried and continue to negatively influence their lives. Sometimes the secret is finally told when a survivor has reached the end of a cycle of self-destructive, punishing behaviors which she cannot continue if she is to survive. Sometimes a survivor decides to tell the secret because she knows that it must be told if she is to put the memory behind her and go on with her life in a positive, productive way.

Every time a survivor breaks her silence, refuses to remain a victim of the sexual abuse cycle, and shares her experience with others, she in some way enables other women to do the same. And, more importantly, she is helping to insure that her victimization will not become self-perpetuating, that she will probably not participate even unknowingly in the victimization of another. The process of prevention and healing all begins with the important first step of telling the secret.

Coping Skills

Unfortunately, not much attention has been focused upon the coping skills of the adult survivor of childhood sexual abuse. Much has been written about their deficiencies: the fact that they experience depression, have difficulty forming and maintaining healthy interpersonal relationships, oftentimes become substance abusers, are self-destructive and even suicide-prone. The negative consequences of childhood sexual abuse cannot be minimized and can never, under any circumstances, be seen as positive, even when survivors have managed to transcend their pain and accomplish incredible things in their lives.

However, when a woman survives one of the most difficult and painful experiences in her life; when she manages to somehow maintain her sanity in the face of tremendous conflicting messages and negative beliefs about herself; when she is betrayed and violated by the most trusted person in her life, and yet survives, she gains a strength that can be an invaluable resource for the rest of her life. Usually a survivor does not see herself as a strong, resourceful person. She images herself as weak and powerless, damaged in most important ways. By taking responsibility for the abuse, which most victims do, a survivor confuses herself and her innate qualities with the inappropriateness and negativity of the sexual abuse, for which she actually bears no responsibility whatsoever. The strengths a survivor has developed are buried and repressed in much the same way as the secret of the abuse has been buried.

But just as it is important to recognize and deal with the issues that create problems in a survivor's life, it is equally, if not more, important to identify in what ways a survivor is resourceful and where her strengths lie. Enduring the anguish, the pain, and the confusion of childhood sexual abuse teaches a victim the art of survival—a learning experience that will help her surmount many obstacles in her life once she recognizes her strengths and relies upon them to survive just as she survived her abuse.

Stuckness

Many survivors of childhood sexual abuse remain stuck even after having engaged in therapy and worked long and hard to get on with their lives. Although they express frustration at this stuckness and want desperately to move forward, they can't seem to break out of their cycle of pain and dysfunction. One of the reasons for the immobility on the part of the adult survivor is that it's difficult to move on when a large piece of the work remains unfinished. Most survivors, while they have accepted the limitations of their dysfunctional family of origin and may have sufficiently worked through the anger and disappointment they feel for their abusers, still cling to the fantasy that they will get what they need from their families. Some women believe they need the acknowledgement that they were victimized and hurt, along with an apology from the abuser. Some believe they need their mothers, who failed to intervene and to protect them from the abuse, to admit that they knew of the abuse and were wrong in not stopping it. Many women feel that they were robbed of their childhood and want somehow to regain what they lost.

Most victims long for a family that is nurturing, protective, loving and kind. Having failed to get all those things and more from their families, they remain rooted in the fantasy that somehow, some way they will get what they need—and as a result they fail to move on with their lives. As much as they want to go forward, it is hard for survivors to trust that things can be better before they have received from their families all that one is supposed to receive from a healthy, caring family.

Anger

Sexual abuse survivors have great difficulty recognizing and expressing their rage. Children are not encouraged to be angry at their parents or caretakers, and children who are sexually abused are discouraged even more from expressing displeasure. They are forced to endure the confusion, the pain, the negative feelings that they have, and to repress them. Anger, after all, is an emotion that churns things up, creates a distance between people. Sexual abuse victims aren't allowed that distance. So, victims of child abuse don't speak of their anger, if indeed they can recognize and feel it, and they don't learn how to effectively use anger in their lives.

Anger is a threatening emotion for victims, one that would cause the equilibrium, the homeostasis of the sexual-abuse family to become unbalanced. And it is important for the balance to be maintained. On some level victims of sexual abuse know this and "cooperate." They play out their role as compliant victims and continually put their anger down, keeping it in a private place—unexpressed and unresolved. When adult survivors find themselves subsequently in situations where they are being violated, both in large and small ways, they usually can call upon some mechanism of defense that allows them to deny the reality of their violation. Many will accept their abuse passively, as they learned to do in the past, because to respond in an angry, self-protective, and powerful way is not within their frame of reference.

It is particularly difficult for women in our society to express anger. It is not considered feminine or nurturing, and, in addition, it creates conflict. Conflict, at best, is difficult to deal with and to resolve, requiring skills of power and control, appropriately channeled anger, and the willingness to lose. These qualities do not come easily to the adult survivor of sexual abuse, and the expression of anger poses the greatest challenge. A survivor must give herself permission to be angry. Once she has explored the extent of her pain and given voice to her rage, she will gradually begin to heal from the injuries she has suffered and no longer have to accept them silently.

Boundries

Boundaries are an important part of the structure of our lives. They tell us how far it is safe to go. They provide for us an area that is defined and understood, and they keep us from entering places where we do not belong.

In a family where sexual abuse occurs, the boundaries are blurred or nonexistent. The people responsible for creating and maintaining healthy and appropriate boundaries, the primary caretakers, cannot or will not do so. Indeed, if boundaries had been established and utilized, sexual abuse likely would not have taken place. The boundaries that are available and necessary for children raised in a healthy family are not available to victims of sexual abuse. As a result of growing up in a family with non-existent or blurred boundaries, the child victim develops without an awareness and a knowledge of boundaries and of how important they are to maintaining relationships and protecting them from injury.

The absence of boundaries can also cause a victim who feels frightened and unprotected to establish personal boundaries that are restrictive, rigid and inflexible. The victim may feel safer and less vulnerable but end up needing to maintain this control at all costs. A great deal of energy is expended holding these boundaries in place. Not much is let out and even less is allowed in. Eventually these impenetrable boundaries can become prisons, safe and predictable, but prisons nonetheless.

Dissociation

Dissociation is a defense used by many victims of trauma in order to survive the pain of their experience. Some sexual abuse victims have been able to use dissociation very effectively and to split off parts of themselves that are too difficult to own. They are able to compartmentalize their thoughts and their feelings, to become separated from themselves and to keep the bad in one place and the good in another. It is theorized by some that those victims who are unable to dissociate from their painful experiences are those people most likely to abuse substances such as alcohol and other drugs to dull the pain or help them to forget altogether. Other self-destructive behaviors may also be part of a victim's attempt to survive or escape her pain, including thinking about or attempting suicide.

While it is necessary for a victim of trauma to use a number of defenses, including dissociation, in order to survive her negative experiences, these same defenses are an obstacle to a person who wishes to become fully integrated, whole, and capable of feeling pain and pleasure alike. Dissociation is an ally to a victim who cannot escape or change her situation, but once she survives the experience and wishes to engage fully in life, dissociation can keep her from reaching her goal.

Sexual Abuse by an Extended Family Member

Many women report being sexually victimized by a member of their extended family such as their grandfather, uncle, cousin, or a host of others. In many instances the victim had a relationship with the perpetrator that could be characterized as close and trusting. Women who have been victimized by these family members usually react in much the same way as those women who were victimized within their immediate families. They felt compelled to "keep the secret," thereby protecting the abuser. These children often feel responsible for the abuse, and guilty because they believed they provoked it. Frequently they are reluctant to tell their parents or caretakers of the offense because they know revealing it will hurt them and cause a rift in the relationship between all parties. All too often their fears are realized when they tell their parents of their abuse and they are ignored, not believed or punished for "causing trouble."

The message to the victim when this happens is, "You're all alone in this. You are powerless to do anything about it or have anyone else value you enough to intervene." It's no wonder victims who are not supported and protected when they tell of their abuse grow up learning not to depend on anyone else to satisfy their needs or protect them from danger. This experience of isolation also teaches the young victim how to distance herself emotionally from people and create her own world, from which she may never emerge.

The consequences of "keeping the secret" are similar to those experienced by victims abused within their families. One of the major differences, however, is that the victim's immediate family may be healthier and more stable since the abuse did not occur within the family. This healthy, stable family can provide a context for the abuse victim within which she will continue to grow and develop. Her pain and disappointment, her sense of isolation as she holds onto the knowledge of her abuse while not sharing it with her family, will all still have a tremendous impact upon the victim. However, she has a better chance of learning ways of dealing with the world by growing up in a relatively healthy family than does the victim who comes from a dysfunctional, abusive family.

Sometimes a victim will choose to report the sexual offense to her parents or caretakers. In my experience this generally happens when the victim knows on some level that her caretakers will respond appropriately by becoming angry, doing something to insure her safety, and confronting the perpetrator. The message that the victim receives in this situation is a positive one. She learns that what happened to her wasn't her fault. She learns that her parents are willing to take action to protect her and to insure that the perpetrator is punished for the wrongdoing. The victim is often helped to get the therapy she needs in order to more fully comprehend the situation and heal from its effects.

When all of this happens, the victim has an excellent chance of recovering from the devastation of sexual abuse by a family member outside the immediate family. She frequently does not have to suffer from the trauma of her abuse for the rest of her life but can go forward with the love and support of her immediate family. Her trust level may be somewhat weakened, which will influence her subsequent relationships, but she will have as a balance in her life the knowledge that there are people who value and support her through both the good and the not-so-good times.

Issues for Women
Sexually Abused Outside Their Families

Women who were sexually abused or assaulted by someone outside their immediate family share many of the same problems as those women abused by a family member or caretaker. However, there are a few differences in both the reaction of victims to their abuse and the effects they experience that need to be noted. One overriding issue for victims of abuse is that of the response or nonresponse of other people, generally parents and caretakers, to the victim's experience. The reactions of those responsible for the well-being of the victimized youngster determine in large measure the effects of the abuse on the victim.

For all victims of abuse, whether within or outside their families, the loss of trust and hope is crushing and debilitating. However, the intensity and longevity of the negative consequences of sexual victimization are determined in large measure by the response of the victim's support system. If a victim is given the opportunity to heal in a safe, supportive and sympathetic environment, the possibilities for her are enhanced. If a victim is revictimized by blame and anger, or if her victimization is minimized or even denied, then her chances for healing are lessened.

In order for anyone to grow and develop, to take important and necessary risks in life, there needs to be a firm belief that the world, although hurtful on occasion, is generally a safe place in which to live. This feeling of safety or trust is a crucial one, and one that determines whether an individual will continue to challenge the world or become immobilized.

Sexual Victimization by a Stranger

Sexual abuse within the family is a much more common occurrence than is abuse by a stranger, but since it does happen, it needs to be included in our discussion of victimization. Again, in this situation the response of the victim and the prognosis for healing are highly related to the reaction of the partners or caretakers. If the parents are supportive of the victim and do whatever is in their power to help her to heal from the abuse, she has an excellent chance of recovery. What the victim must deal with, what all victims of random and senseless violence have to deal with, is the shattering of her belief that the world is a safe and sane place to be. This disillusionment colors the life of the victimized person forever. The experience of victimization robs the victim of an innocence about the world forever. It creates a wound and a scar that will never go away.

Some victims use this negative experience to help educate others about exercising caution in dealing with the world. They use their pain and trauma to help others avoid being victimized. It becomes a way in which to reframe an otherwise terrible and senseless experience in their lives. This is a powerful component for healing which you will learn more about as you meet some of the women in this book who have been victimized.

Sexual Abuse by a Helping Professional

More and more we are hearing about the sexual victimization of young children, boys and girls alike, by those who are supposed to be committed to their welfare. These can be people such as Boy Scout leaders, doctors, religious leaders, and any number of individuals whom parents trust to guide and teach their children.

The violation of their position and the trust of the children they are committed to help is unconscionable. The major trauma in this type of abuse is very similar to that in any abuse perpetrated by a trusted person: the destroying of trust. When children grow to rely on and believe in an individual, to look to them for certain things, and are then sexually victimized by this person, their trust is shattered. The violation is compounded when the abuser seems to represent values such as God, moral and ethical behavior, truth, justice, and "the American way."

It's not unusual for such a victim to reject, often forever, what the victimizer claimed to represent and was responsible for teaching. It's very difficult for a young victim to understand the hypocrisy of someone purporting to represent certain values and standards while they are committing grievous acts upon a child.

The Family as Victim

When a woman is a victim of incest, the perpetrator of the abuse is a member of the family or someone who has assumed the role of caretaker. This family is generally dysfunctional and the incest is a way to contain the dysfunction and maintain a semblance of stability. Sometimes family members either consciously or unconsciously collude in the incest to insure survival of the family unit. Incestuous families very often deny their pain, dissociate from their feelings of inadequacy, and fail to acknowledge the burden the victim of incest must bear for the system.

When a woman is the victim of a random act of sexual assault or is violated by someone outside the family, either known or unknown to the family, none of this applies. The family of the woman who has been victimized then becomes part of the trauma she has suffered and join her in the experience of rage, pain, and, hopefully, recovery.

The family usually feels initially that something has been taken from them; that someone has entered their "home" and has robbed them of their loved one. They feel violated and angry. The circle of safety and protection that they had carefully constructed around their family member has been permeated and they will never trust the world quite as much ever again.

Another common reaction for the family of the victim is that of guilt. Why couldn't they prevent this terrible thing from happening to their daughter or sister? If the abuse had been perpetrated by someone in close proximity, such as a neighbor or friend, why didn't they see it or at least pick up the subtle signs that this was happening? The guilt is compounded if the child came to them with fears and anxieties about the abuser that they discounted or rebuffed. Even now when we've heard so many stories of sexual victimization perpetrated by family members, doctors, priests, ministers, neighbors, and a host of others, we have difficulty believing that this kind of thing can happen. It's almost too much to comprehend that someone could sexually molest or rape an innocent and lovely child. We build up defenses to protect us from letting these awful truths enter our thoughts and destroy our belief that the world is a safe and a good place to be, especially for children.

When a family learns that their child was sexually assaulted, invariably they experience feelings of guilt in addition to the anger. All their efforts to be good and protective parents were unsuccessful. They feel that they have failed their daughter as parents or failed their sister as a brother or a sister. Oftentimes parents then call into question all the other things they did over the course of their parenting that may prove to be inadequate or insufficient.

The family system is rocked when a member has been victimized. The pain and the devastation the victim feels is shared by each family member, and in this sense, the entire family can be viewed as "the victim" of a traumatic event.

The hope for recovery for the victim and her family lies in the ability of the family to join with one another as they work towards healing, both as individuals and as a family unit. The victim goes through a process of dealing with feelings of being violated and hurt. Her choice was taken away by another, and she needs to learn how to take back her life and her choices. She needs to feel strong again and to be able to reframe this event so that she has control of what happens to her as much as possible. Her family should be supportive of her efforts and provide for her the love and the support she needs to recover.

The family needs to work through their individual issues of rage and guilt and feelings of being inadequate. Oftentimes this is done in therapy as a complete family unit so that other members of the family can be aware and sensitive to each others pain. However the process occurs, people need to express their feelings and to help one another as they try to put the pain behind them and to go on with a renewed sense of strength and commitment to each other and to the family.

Families share many life events. Together they celebrate holidays and birthdays and other momentous occasions. They weave the fabric of their lives over a span of many years with the threads of laughter and tears, of joy and sorrow. The color of their happiness is bright and rich, their sadness is dark and heavy. Their tapestry is a contrast of many colors and many experiences they have shared with one another as a family. The trauma of sexual victimization is one which will be woven together with all the other threads and must be seen by the family as something that together they can triumph over and perhaps become stronger because they were joined in a very powerful and profound way.

Ending The Cycle

Fortunately many people are beginning to come forward and talk about the abuse they suffered from adults who were either family members, strangers, or helping professionals. Because of the courage of these survivors, society is beginning to take seriously the problem of sexual victimization. It's hard not to respond empathetically to a person who tells about the trauma they experienced as a victim and the resulting dysfunction they suffered that took a heavy toll on their health and well-being.

We've come to realize just how many lives have been affected by the crime of sexual abuse. Experts tell us that one out of four women will be sexually abused before they reach the age of eighteen. The figures for young men are said to be one out of six. However, there are some researchers who claim that girls and boys are abused in about the same numbers.

What we do know is that there is a terrible price to pay if this problem continues. All you have to do is pick up a newspaper and read of some ghastly crime that has been committed by a perpetrator who was abused as a child to know that sexual, physical, and emotional abuse of children has a devastating impact both upon the victim and upon society.

The cycle of abuse must end, and we can all be part of ending that cycle. Even if all we do is learn more about the issue and become more sensitive to the trauma that victims suffer, we will have been part of shedding light on this awful problem and making it more difficult for it to continue. Sexual abuse of children is not the kind of aberration that has the characteristics of a disease. Sexual abuse victims and survivors, for the most part, look whole and healthy. There are no telethons for victims or poster children looking at us with doleful eyes, but we are beginning to recognize how devastating this problem is to it's victims. That's a beginning.

QUESTIONNAIRE

Step 1   Know the consequences of your abuse.

If you were sexually abused as a child, which of the following issues have been a problem for you as an adult?

Telling the Secret	_____	Choice	_____
Boundaries	_____	Intimacy	_____
Dissociation	_____	Anger	_____
Coping Skills	_____	Stuckness	_____

Were you sexually abused outside your family through:

Date rape? _____

Extended family member?_____

      (Who?) _____

Stranger? _____

Helping professional?_____

Did you report the abuse to:

Someone in authority? _____
    (ie. school administration)

Police? _____

Family member?_____

Professional licensing board? _____

What was the response? _____

_____

_____

_____

How did this response or lack of response affect your life?

_____

_____

_____

    Reporting sexual abuse, rape, or any sexual victimization is not easy, but for some women it helps them to claim or reclaim their power. If you have any questions about reporting your victimization, call your local Rape Crisis Center, Hotline, or Women's Center for advice and guidance. They will provide you with important information and support. The choice is yours.

The Power of Healing

2

Childhood sexual abuse used to be covered by a cloak of secrecy. Denial about the fact that adult caretakers were violating the children they were responsible for protecting and nurturing kept sexual abuse in the shadows of society. As a sad consequence of our reluctance to admit that this awful problem existed and existed in large magnitude, survivors were not afforded the opportunity to heal from their trauma. Their personal sense of isolation and the mistaken belief that they were responsible for the abuse, reinforced survivors for holding onto the secret of their abusive pasts. In many instances, adult survivors buried the pain of their victimization so deeply and so thoroughly that even the memories of their pasts were locked away, unavailable to them. This protective mechanism that served to protect the child victim and adult survivor from unspeakable pain also blocked survivors from the facts of their lives. Caught in cycles of inappropriate behaviors, abusive relationships, and overwhelming fears, survivors searched for answers to why their lives seemed fractured and fragmented.

Gradually survivors began to retrieve their memories and share their experiences as victims. Sometimes they talked to therapists, oftentimes they talked to one another, but most importantly, they talked and listened to themselves. The puzzle of their lives began to take shape and to explain in large measure why they behaved as they did and what they needed to do to recover from their wounds. Therapists began to learn more about the devastating effects of sexual abuse and to guide survivors through a therapeutic process that has offered hope and healing to them at long last.

Hopefully, this chapter offers information that will be helpful to therapists and to survivors who seek to become more aware of the connection between their early victimization, the ways in which it influenced their lives, and how they can continue to grow stronger and become more powerful each day.

This chapter also offers a perspective to those who want to enhance their knowledge and awareness of the issues that sexual abuse survivors deal with in their lives. As survivors have shared the truth of their lives, helping professionals have been able to focus on the right issues, understand their clients more fully, and to provide the most effective and appropriate treatment. Both male and female therapists, if they are skilled and knowledgeable, sensitive and aware, can provide effective therapy for a female adult survivor of sexual abuse. The following information that deals with the relationship between therapist and survivor, therefore, will reflect both genders in as balanced a way as possible.

Telling the Secret

The first step in the process of healing is generally the most difficult and important one. For a survivor of childhood sexual abuse, telling the secret is very painful and filled with complexities that usually don't apply to other issues the therapist is accustomed to dealing with. A therapist must reassure the survivor from the outset that she did the right thing in breaking her silence. She needs to be told that she is no longer a passive, powerless victim, she is no longer the child who needs to keep the secret of her abuse to keep her family intact. She no longer needs to bear the shame, the guilt, the pain of sexual abuse. In fact, to do so means remaining stuck in a dynamic that is destructive, negative, and not conducive to her emotional well-being. Most importantly, the survivor needs to be assured that she is no longer alone in her confusion and pain.

The message that the survivor did the best possible thing for herself in breaking the silence will help her to internalize this attitude and to, hopefully, reject any thoughts that she has betrayed her family and her abuser. She is, in fact, advocating for herself in a very powerful and productive way which will bode well for her future mental and emotional health.

It is extremely hard for a sexual abuse survivor to break the bonds of the past, to see herself with new eyes as a worthwhile person, entitled to a normal, happy life, capable of forming healthy relationships and deserving of them. A therapist should constantly give feedback to the survivor about her strengths. Many times a survivor will focus upon her deficits and fail to recognize and appreciate her positive qualities. She needs to be reminded in therapy that she has great courage to pursue a life that does not require her to be a victim anymore. Throughout the counseling process, the therapist should continually reinforce the positive images and beliefs she has about the survivor. The therapist may be the first person in her life who knows the survivor's secret of her sexual abuse, who has heard the details that have caused her so much anxiety and pain, and who values and affirms her.

A survivor will often try to give her therapist an "overview" of the abuse, to speak in general terms and then quickly leap to the process of healing. As painful as it may be for both the therapist and the survivor to speak of the details of the survivor's abuse, it must be done and done as completely as possible. Any part of the secret that is kept hidden, no matter how small, may fester and keep the survivor from being totally free of the abuse. It's not uncommon for a survivor to feel that if her secret is revealed, if anyone knows all that can be known about her, she will be rejected, held in contempt, judged harshly, and, most importantly, not be able to offer anything in her own defense. As the survivor breaks her silence in therapy and finds her therapist to be understanding and nonjudgmental, her fears are dissipated and she is encouraged to continue the process.

However, because the survivor has held on for so long to the myth of her "badness," her therapist should be prepared for the survivor to exhibit self-destructive behavior once the secret has been told. For years the survivor has been loyal to her family by keeping the secret of her abuse. By telling the secret, the survivor almost always will experience a deep sense of guilt for which she feels she deserves to be punished. Because the family is not able to mete out that punishment, and because the survivor has typically taken upon herself much of the responsibility for the family, she may punish herself for her disloyalty. If her therapist is aware of this possibility, he can insure that the survivor has a net of safety as she breaks her silence for the first time.

The survivor of sexual abuse needs in her life at least one person for whom she has respect and trust, who knows her in depth, is aware of her past, and who does not waver in the belief that she is a valuable and fine person. Her therapist can be that person and, hopefully, the catalyst for the survivor to form many other satisfying and reciprocal relationships. All of this begins when she takes the first important step of breaking her silence and begins the process of healing in her life.

Choice

One of the most powerful tools of a therapist who is beginning to work with an adult survivor is the fact that she made the choice to talk about her abuse and to begin the process of recovering from the experience. This is a strong move, a move that should be reinforced, particularly when the survivor begins to fall back into old thinking about not having choices in her life. Whatever serves to break the cycle of powerlessness for a survivor, however small a move, is important. If her therapist reinforces and validates her for making choices in her life, the adult survivor will gradually begin to take control of her life and direct it as *she* chooses.

In counseling there are numerous ways in which a survivor can exercise choice and have a new learning experience. These choices are best negotiated and agreed upon, as much as possible, so that the survivor learns something about the process of negotiating. This process will include compromise and acceptance of the fact that nobody has control of the situation all the time. For instance, the areas in which choices are appropriate and negotiable are: fee schedule, appointment scheduling, and structure of the session, to name a few. Information about the treatment approach and strategies certainly should be available to the survivor so that she can make an informed choice about her treatment, but the client does not determine the treatment. The therapist ultimately has the responsibility for providing treatment based on her expertise, her skills, and the nature of the contract that was agreed upon by both the client and the therapist. The survivor, of course, should choose whether or not she wishes to participate, and should be made to feel comfortable with whatever choice she makes. A survivor who is beginning to exercise choice in her life needs to be reinforced for her behavior while at the same time learning that some choices are appropriately hers and some are not. This may prove to be an area of tension in therapy for a survivor who is discovering her personal power, but it can provide an excellent opportunity for positive change.

As so often happens, when an individual makes the decision to change, especially when these changes are powerful and deliberate, others react to these changes. The therapist will probably need to spend a good deal of time supporting the survivor as she deals with the impact her life has on other people and the pressure that may ensue. It has been said that the only people who like change are wet babies. There is always a price to pay for change, and the therapist will need to help the survivor continually reassess her decision to become different, to no longer be a victim. The therapist should closely look for the positive payoffs for survivorship and help the survivor appreciate those changes in her life. The therapist should reassure the survivor that it is not easy to reverse a lifetime of learning and behaviors—but that the rewards are worth the effort and the choice is hers.

Boundaries

One of the most important tasks of the therapist is to model for the survivor how to form appropriate and healthy boundaries and maintain them. This may be a new learning experience for the survivor of sexual abuse and one which may be difficult to achieve, given the fact that boundaries must be firm to be effective but flexible to avoid rigid, fixed behavior.

It is important for the therapist to understand the issues of boundaries as they apply to the adult survivor. It is not uncommon for a therapist to be tested by the survivor of sexual abuse as to where the boundaries begin and end. If the therapist is at all uncertain himself, he will be forced to make up the boundaries as he goes along, which is never a preferred style. If the therapist is to be helpful to the survivor, he must engage with her while maintaining appropriate and healthy boundaries. A therapist is trained to respect the client's boundaries and must make boundary issues a top priority when working with a survivor of sexual abuse. For the survivor of sexual abuse, this is such an important part of her therapy that it is imperative the therapist take the time once more to objectively establish his own personal/professional boundaries and to value them as one of the most important therapeutic experiences he can share with the survivor.

In many cases the survivor may distance herself from her therapist. Intimacy and closeness is threatening to her, given her experience of being sexually abused. This chasm may be frustrating and create anxiety for the therapist. It may even cause the therapist to become angry, especially if he repeatedly has reached out to join with his client, to show her that he cares about her pain and wants to help her, and is constantly rebuffed. He may feel that he is doing all the work—and perhaps he is. However, impatience and frustration might cause even the most skilled therapist to cross a line, violate a boundary, repeat the abuse in yet another setting. If the survivor keeps her therapist outside her personal, emotional space, at least she's working on her boundary issues. With skill and patience, the therapist will, hopefully, be able to show his client that if she allows him to get close, she will not be harmed and be a victim yet again.

Intimacy

The inability of a sexual abuse survivor to feel comfortable in an intimate relationship or to enjoy a fulfilling, dynamic sexual relationship is oftentimes the motivation for her to seek treatment. While she may consider the fact that intimacy can be a pleasant experience, she generally wishes to be released from the ambivalence, discomfort, and pain of intimacy. Her memories of "intimacy," after all, are not positive and have been the source of most of her unhappiness and dysfunction.

Generally, the relationship that a therapist needs to establish in order to help his client help herself is a very intimate one, and that creates a particular level of anxiety for the survivor. It is helpful for the therapist to point out to the survivor that he understands her reluctance to engage in a close relationship, that her experiences as a victim of sexual abuse caused her to form negative attitudes, develop intense fears, and resist intimate behavior. Her attitudes, however, are based on past history, and once she has dealt with the abuse, she should be able to form and maintain intimate relationships.

A particular problem for a survivor of sexual abuse is that of participation. Many children, because they did not say "no" to the abuse and "complied" with the abuser, however reluctantly, believed that they participated in the abuse. The reality is that child victims do not participate or collude in their abuse. It *happened* to them through no fault or responsibility on their part. An adult, consenting relationship is completely different, and once they can accept that difference, they can separate sexual abuse from healthy sexual activity with the partner of their choice.

A therapist should *continually* remind the survivor of the reality of the present situation; helping her to believe that she can put the painful experience of sexual abuse behind her in order to live the normal life to which she is entitled. In many cases, it helps to include the partner in this phase of treatment once the survivor feels comfortable advocating for herself, and does not continue to carry the guilt and shame for her abuse.

Working on the issue of intimacy is an excellent place to break the cycle of abuse. The survivor finally has an opportunity to speak of her discomfort with intimacy and to find alternative ways to deal with it. In the past, she had no choice but to comply and to maintain her silence. Now she can do something different, with the help of her therapist, and have the chance to live a full, rich life where intimacy is not only possible but pleasurable.

Dissociation

As a sexual abuse survivor begins to speak of her abuse, her therapist may notice how skillfully she is able to separate thought from feeling, to create a mind/body split. The dissociation that she relied upon to escape the pain of the situation when she was being victimized as a child is a technique she continues to use when she feels threatened.

When a therapist works with a survivor who splits thought from feeling, the therapist may think that he is dealing with two people; the feeling person and the cognitive or thinking person. Usually the cognitive person, who can be safer and more in control, is the one who emerges in therapy. It is important to remember that while therapists are trained to encourage clients to express their feelings, their pain, their unresolved issues, this requires an openness and a vulnerability. Sexual abuse survivors have great difficulty being vulnerable. The therapist can be very instrumental in modeling for the survivor that vulnerability and strength can co-exist and indeed complement one another. An adult survivor can be helped to learn that to be vulnerable does not always put one at risk of harm. It is crucial for adult survivors to learn that when one has developed a personal sense of power, vulnerability can become a safe option. This can be accomplished in the individual therapy stage and perhaps be further developed within group treatment with other survivors who have known the same fear of being victimized when they are vulnerable.

If an adult survivor feels safer when she is in a cognitive mode, her therapist can work with that part of her until she is ready to let her vulnerable, frightened child tell him how she feels, how it felt to be abused and to be powerless to stop it. Patience is a therapist's best ally as he works with the adult side of the adult survivor of sexual abuse who keeps her frightened child, the child who was violated and hurt, safe from harm.

Eventually, the therapist can help his client see that dissociation can be a valuable defense and an important resource when she uses it during times of her life that are appropriate—a visit to the dentist perhaps, but inappropriate when she needs to feel pain and pleasure, fully human and capable of feeling and expressing a wide range of human emotion. The key is to be able to exercise choice wisely. Dissociation can be a powerful coping skill and a strength when it is under the control of the survivor. In therapy a survivor can explore ways to exercise control over dissociative behavior and not let it be her only defensive strategy and an obstacle to a complete experience of life.

Anger

A sexual abuse survivor oftentimes will not be able to express her anger at her abuser until she is nearing the end of her treatment. In fact, it is usually the finishing piece and a sign that the survivor may not repeat her role as victim in the future. However, a therapist may find that the anger a survivor feels at the mother or mother figure who should have intervened and protected her from the abuse, will emerge at the beginning phase of the treatment. It is safer to be angry at the person the victim won't be in danger of losing. In most cases the relationship with the mother was distant or empty from the beginning, and it's hard to lose something you never had.

There are two important components that need to be in place for a survivor before she can begin to deal with her anger. First, a survivor must be at a point where she has gained self-esteem and believes that she is entitled to express all the feelings she has without judgment and without censure, either from herself or from her therapist. Secondly, a survivor must be free of the guilt she carries for the abuse and must be helped to recognize that she was not responsible for the abuse, that the abuser bears the TOTAL responsibility. Children have difficulty admitting that their parents may be bad or wrong so when they are abused, they take upon themselves the guilt that belongs to the perpetrator and are confused about who and what to be angry at.

From the beginning, the therapist needs to continually reassure the survivor that she didn't do anything wrong; the abuse was wrong, not the victim of the abuse. This reassurance, along with the therapist's concern and his commitment to the survivor, will help her to see herself as a valuable, worthwhile person. Helping a survivor as she seeks to raise her self-esteem is a long and difficult task, but one that is crucial if a survivor is to feel entitled to her anger and to recovery and healing.

In many instances, a survivor directs her anger inward. Unable to verbalize her feelings of dissatisfaction, if indeed she recognizes them, she redirects her anger from the abuser and the situation that created the abuse and focuses it upon herself. Anger is an energizing force. When directed appropriately towards a person or event that is problematic, the result may be a resolution of the problem or at best a diffusion of the energy that fuels the anger. When a sexual abuse survivor begins to express her anger, she is making positive strides towards placing the responsibility with the responsible party. It also means that she is required to give up the responsibility she has assumed for the abuse. This is oftentimes a difficult transfer to make, especially when she realizes that being responsible has payoffs. It may be a skewed and inappropriate way to feel necessary and important, but it nonetheless was, and probably still is, a large part of the persona of the survivor. The therapist's job is to help the survivor find or recognize more appropriate ways in which she is important—her job, her interpersonal relationships, her involvement in the community. Gradually, the survivor will begin to feel competent and powerful for the positive, healthy things in her life. She will find that she no longer needs or wants to be a victim for anyone in order to believe that she has a valuable role to fulfill in her life and the lives of others.

Coping Skills

A therapist who works with an adult survivor of sexual abuse becomes aware of the negative consequences of the abuse and of how it has affected the survivor's life. This knowledge will help the therapist effectively counsel the survivor and focus upon the right issues. A therapist discovers the source of the survivor's pain and how the sexual abuse has impacted her life, influenced her choices and determined the kinds of relationships of which she has been a part.

If a therapist, however, fails to see the strengths of the survivor and to build upon them immediately as she begins to work, she is missing the most important resource. As a result of her abuse, the adult survivor of childhood sexual abuse has developed a number of coping skills that helped her to survive one of the most horrendous experiences an individual can know. From the moment the adult survivor engages with the therapist, the therapist should pay close attention to the resources the survivor possesses and call attention to them. The survivor may not easily own her strengths. After all, she has fostered a negative image of herself for some time. Her identity was formed from a number of messages she received from people she trusted to be correct in their assessment of her. Most of these messages were not positive or self-enhancing. The therapist is attempting to change all that and to cause the survivor to see herself in a different, more positive light. This may be very difficult for the survivor, but the therapist's willingness to call forth her strengths and her power and to reinforce them for her benefit, will help the survivor to see herself not as a victim any longer but as someone who is capable of exercising power and control over her life using the strengths she developed as she survived her victimization.

A therapist can help the survivor see in what ways she has transcended her abuse and to appreciate her power even when she is unable to do so herself. By reminding her that she is a survivor—not a victim—eventually the survivor may join her therapist in knowing how special she really is. When that happens, when the survivor realizes that some terrible things happened to her but that she is and always has been a good person, the survivor may no longer be willing to settle for less than she deserves. She will refuse to be a victim any longer in order to help another feel powerful. The survivor will realize that she can make choices in her life that are hers and hers alone. When guilt and shame are put behind her along with the memories of her abuse, the survivor may have reached a point where she can think of herself as a strong, resourceful person who survived her abusive past and is capable of accomplishing much more.

Stuckness

One of the most important things a survivor needs to accomplish in therapy is to become unstuck and give up her fantasy that she will get the things she needs from her family. Many survivors want recognition from their families that they were abused. Many want an apology from a remorseful perpetrator. However, what usually happens when survivors confront their families is that their families deny the abuse, blame the victim, and otherwise fail to take responsibility for the victimization.

The sexual abuse survivor needs to become unstuck from this abusive system if she wants to become an adult survivor and not an adult victim. While the survivor may no longer be a child victim of sexual abuse in her family, she may still be a victim of emotional abuse from her dysfunctional family.

The reality that her family will never be what she wants and needs them to be is a difficult reality to face. It may take some time and effort on the part of the therapist to help the survivor let go of her fantasy. Sometimes the survivor has to admit that she was shortchanged as a child. She may need to face the fact that her family may never get healthy enough to acknowledge her victimization and take the responsibility for it. Most painful of all, the survivor might have to make the decision to move on with her life and give up the hope that she will eventually have the love and support from her family she needed as a child and still needs as an adult.

Her therapist can help her to see that she is remaining a victim by staying stuck and looking to her family for her healing. The therapist can also help her to see the many productive and healthy ways in which she can use her energy instead of trying to make her fantasy come true, a vain hope at best. The therapist can be instrumental in helping the survivor to rechannel her hopes and dreams in ways that are obtainable. After all, the survivor now has choices in her life. She also has discovered the many strengths and coping skills that she developed as a survivor. Most importantly, a survivor can get her needs met, whatever they may be, through her relationships with people who will not abuse and victimize her.

The survivor's family may still be present in her life, she may still have a relationship of sorts with them, but she will no longer have unrealistic expectations of them and will have become unstuck from the "family fantasy." Until that happens, she will not be able to walk away from the abusive family and walk into a new and better life for herself. The therapist can help her to face this difficult reality, to help her grieve the loss of all she never had, and to be with her as she struggles to become unstuck—and to rejoice with her as she moves on to a better life.

These are some of the more important issues that impact sexual abuse survivors. The important thing for therapists to remember is that each survivor brings with her a unique set of dynamics, her own war story. While these issues are important to consider, therapists are continuing to learn more about sexual abuse of children and adult survivors as they come forward in great numbers to share their experiences. Having knowledge about incest and its consequences is vitally important. The next chapter offers more information, some of which might be helpful to those professionals who wish to increase their knowledge and understanding of incest by gaining an historical perspective. We begin by knowing—we end by doing.

QUESTIONNAIRE

Step 2 The step to healing.

Have you been in therapy to deal with your sexual abuse?

Yes _____ No _____

If the answer is Yes, do you feel that you completed the process?

Yes _____ No _____

If you have not been in therapy or feel that you did not complete the process, consider the following:

CHOOSING A THERAPIST

Sometimes you can get the name of a competent therapist from a friend or family member. If a referral is made to you in this way, ask the following:

- Why did you like this therapist?
- Do you feel that you benefited from being in therapy with this person?
  Did you accomplish what you hoped to accomplish with this therapist?
- Are there any negatives I should know about this therapist?
- Ask those questions that are of particular importance to you, i.e., did your therapist keep you waiting? Was your therapist directive in offering suggestions for change? Does your therapist work with couples?

If you need the name of a therapist who specializes in childhood sexual abuse, you can call the following sources for a referral:

- Your local Rape Crisis Center, Battered Women's Shelter, the Women's Center at your local college or university, The Society for Prevention of Cruelty to Children, your local mental health center, your physician, the United Way, the American Psychological Association in your city or state, the American Association of Marriage and Family Therapists in your city or state.

Once you have the name of a therapist, find out the following information:

- If you have insurance, who is the carrier? What is the deductible? Does the insurance cover out-patient psychological counseling? What is the co-pay or amount that you are responsible for paying (for instance, some policies cover 50 percent of the counselor's fee, some policies cover 80 percent. Some policies cover a percentage of a certain rate such as 80 percent of $75.)

- Is your insurance an HMO (Health Maintenance Organization)? If you have an HMO, you are generally limited as to whom you can choose for therapy. You may have to make a choice of those therapists who are part of the HMO system. Some HMOs will allow you to "go out of the system" if they do not provide the specialty you require, or if you have prior approval from your primary physician. Get all this information from your HMO.

The important thing is to find out what you have for insurance coverage if you plan to use your insurance for counseling.

Once you have made the choice of therapist, call for an appointment, and be prepared to ask those questions that are important to you. Always remember that you are the consumer and you have the right to determine what kind of health care you are going to be provided. The following questions are suggested, but everyone has her own criteria for choosing a therapist:

- What is the educational background and training of the therapist?
- How long has the therapist been practicing?
- Does the therapist take appointments that are compatible with your schedule? (i.e., evenings, Saturdays).
- Does the therapist have a sliding fee schedule based on your income?

During the initial interview with the therapist, you should ask those questions that have to do with the process.

- Will we contract for a certain amount of weeks or months?
- Will what I tell you in therapy be strictly confidential?
- Ask any other question you have about the process of therapy.

If you do not feel comfortable with the therapist for any reason, you might express your discomfort and try to resolve it during the first session. If you are unable to do that, you can tell the therapist that you do not feel that you can make an appointment at this time. Whatever you do, don't feel that you have to continue working with the therapist if it doesn't seem like a good match. Choose a person who you can work with or you won't accomplish in therapy what you need to.

If you can't afford counseling, there are resources that you can take advantage of to get the help you need:

• Some people go to their minister, rabbi, priest or other religious leader for counseling. This usually does not entail a fee.

• There are some community mental health agencies or clinics that have a very low fee. The United Way will be able to direct you as they subsidize some agencies and award grants for various programs.

• Your local newspaper usually has a listing of the support groups in your area. Many of them are offered for no charge or a minimum fee.

If you need help in dealing with your childhood victimization and either cannot get into counseling or choose not to do so for your own personal reason, you can refer to the reading list at the back of the book and find a self-help book. Therapy is a choice. It is very helpful to a great many people, particularly if the therapist is skilled and knowledgeable. Each individual must do what she needs to do to heal from the trauma of sexual victimization. The choice is yours.

The Power of Knowledge

3

So far this book has focused upon power. It's important for adult survivors to understand as much as they can about power and how they can use and maintain it in their lives. This chapter offers a different kind of power—the power of knowledge. Incest is an issue that we are still struggling to understand. It is something that has been a part of many cultures for a very long time. One thing we've learned is that incest exists primarily in male-dominated or patriarchal societies where power is given to the men and denied to women. This is an important factor to be aware of as it allows us to understand where the seeds of the problem can be found and to possibly change these dynamics in the future. There is other information and sources noted that might be of interest to some readers. Therefore, this chapter briefly offers an historical perspective of incest that will help those who are interested to more fully understand the issue and to have a base for further study.

Incest/childhood sexual abuse is a phenomenon that has occurred in all types of civilizations and in virtually all periods of history. Within the royal families of Greece, Peru, Japan, classical Egypt, and some ruling families in medieval Europe, some forms of incest were deemed acceptable (Henderson, 1975). Incest is defined as sexual contact between a child and an adult who have a parent-child relationship by blood, marriage, or adoption. Sexual companions of a parent (i.e., common-law spouse, boyfriend or girlfriend) are included when the person has functioned as the child's surrogate father, mother, or caretaker. Siblings who initiate sexual activity and/or coerce their sibling into sexual activity are also included in the definition. In broadening the definition of incest, Maltz (1988) adds that an incestuous relationship violates the trust the victim has in a committed relationship. When the needs of the child are unseen and unprotected, and the child is sexually exploited for the satisfaction of the older family person, the emotional bond with the family person is contaminated by secrecy and a feeling of helplessness.

Historical Perspective

Theorists in the disciplines of psychology and anthropology recognize the importance of the incest taboo by characterizing it as a means to discourage inbreeding (Jung, 1916; Lindzey, 1967; Malinowsky, 1927) and a way to control warfare among men (Herman, 1977; Schechner, 1972). Dubreuil (1962) described incest as both a "privilege" and an offense depending upon one's class in society.

One of the earliest references in the literature to incest appeared in 1898 when Westermarck in his *History of Marriage* stated that people who experienced early, prolonged, and intense interaction during early childhood, have an aversion for sexual relations that is present but non-instinctive. It should be noted that the author was referring to sibling incest; the occurrence of parent-child incest was not discussed in the literature until Sigmund Freud, the father of psychoanalytic theory and practice in his *Studies on Hysteria* (1896) admitted the possibility that childhood molestation was etiologic in hysteria.

The Age of Denial

Freud, it appears, initially gave credence to the reports of his patients as they shared with him their histories of incestuous abuse. However, in a letter to Wilhelm Fleiss in 1897, Freud explained how he systematically developed his theories on infantile sexuality and infantile neuroses and rejected the notion of incest which he had originally accepted as a reality. Unwilling to believe that incest was as common as it was in the respected Victorian families of his society, Freud wrote: " . . . it was hardly credible that perverted acts against children were so general." The hysteria which Freud originally attributed to the sexual victimization of young females within their families was subsequently changed to reflect the failure of women to set aside the incestuous fantasies that were present in the Oedipal period of childhood. It was further conjectured that the child's abnormal "constitution" caused the hysteria and unresolved incestuous feelings. Occasionally Freud alluded to seductiveness on the part of the adult but primarily spoke of incest as a childhood developmental issue (Abraham, 1907). As a consequence of Freud's well-constructed abandonment of his clinical experience with incested women and subsequent formulation of theories to explain symptomology in both child and adult populations he treated, the blame for a reality that could not be completely denied was shifted to the victims. This negative attitude towards victims has been a difficult one to overcome as it has existed for a long time and its roots go deep.

Many authors have speculated as to the reason Freud changed his mind about acknowledging that incest was a common theme in families. Some contend that he was afraid to confront his peers, colleagues, friends, and even his own father (Courtois, 1988; Herman, 1983). Consequently, denial about incest pervades the literature and has profoundly affected the response or non-response of professionals to children who complain of sexual behavior with a parent or adult females who report having been sexually violated by a trusted family member.

Some writers during this "Age of Denial," however, did not deny or suppress information they were getting about incest activity in society. Ferenczi (1933), for instance, wrote that childhood seduction was far more common than conventional wisdom or psychoanalytic theory purported. Ferenczi claimed that in order to deal with the psychiatric symptomatology caused by active, sexual molestation, he had to revise this clinical practice and take into account the experiences of his patients who were incest victims. Ferenczi believed that the child's ability to cope and to interact naturally with others was overwhelmed by the serious effects of incestuous activity on ego development. This theory is further supported by Daldin (1988), who contends that "child sexual abuse results in trauma to the developing ego of a child, affecting the individual's future adjustment and adaption so that the capacity to thrive and enjoy life is greatly diminished."

During the '30s, '40s, and early '50s, information was coming forth about incest outside the context of an upper-class private practice. As incest cases were coming to the attention of the legal system, many of the findings concerning childhood sexual abuse were class related (Kaufman, Peck, and Tagiori, 1954). The court cases referred for assistance and treatment involved children of a lower socioeconomic class, and their reaction to the abuse were those of children who appeared to suffer more from general deprivation than sexual molestation (Bender and Blau, 1937). This mingling of psychiatric and legal data tended to focus on who was at fault and led to Bender's conclusion that childhood molestation did not lead to gross dissocial patterns.

Bender's beliefs about the minimal effects of incest contributed to the benign attitudes about incest and further reinforced the denial system that had been so effectively established by Freud. Another influential social commentator who understated the occurrence of incest and kept the issue from being fully explored was Alfred Kinsey. In 1948 when Kinsey published his seminal work, *Sexual Behavior in the Human Male,* only one paragraph in this major and important work was devoted to the subject of incest. Kinsey reported in his study that "the most frequent incestuous contacts are between preadolescent children, but the number of such cases among adolescents or older males is very small" (Kinsey, Pomeroy and Martin, 1948).

By the mid-'50s, a new emphasis appeared in the literature. Kaufman, Peck, and Tagiori (1954) reported their experience in providing treatment to eleven families where incestuous activity had occurred, and wrote of a web of complex interpersonal relationships that involved three generations. The family dynamics that were noted in this study illustrated the growing interest in the social interaction of the family and the multi-generational aspect of incest. Weinberg, a sociologist, was also interested in the types of families in which incest was present. He was less interested in the intrapsychic determinants of incest than in his familial conceptualization, and as a result of Weinberg's study of 203 incestuous families, a classic research document was completed which described a number of family types in which incest was prevalent (Weinberg, 1955). It appears that during this period of time in which denial of the problem was still a problem and blame still rested with the victims when incest was brought to light in a family, some progress was being made in considering the fact that the incest dynamic was a shared family experience.

However, during the '50s, there was a curious mixture of denial that incest existed to any great degree and a growing awareness and recognition of its reality and its sociological/legal/clinical implications. When Freud abandoned his original belief that incest was at the root of the pathology he had observed in many of his patients, most psychiatrists began to assume that either the memories of their own patients when they reported molestation were fantasies or that the child victim had desired the trauma because of a psychological constitution that was abnormal. Litin, Giffen, and Johnson (1956) described the unfortunate effect of this erroneous assumption. They proposed that the denial of the occurrence of incest drove people with an incestuous experience out of therapy, or worse, into psychosis by continually denying the reality of their experience.

Furthering the concept of incest as a symptom of severe family dysfunction opposed to being indicative of a particular type, Cormier, Kennedy and Sangowicz (1962) focused on the psychodynamics of father-daughter incest. The psychiatric literature prior to the 1960s viewed incest as an exotic behavior taking place between retarded, seductive girls and inadequate, sociopathic fathers.

It is apparent at this point that some progress was being made in getting past the denial of incest and that the issue of blame was being reexamined. The child victim was not seen as the protagonist in the incestuous activity but indeed was being viewed as a victim of a dysfunctional family unit. For example, Lustig, Dresser, Spellman, *et al* (1966) had as their express concern the combining of individual and family dynamics in order to understand incest. The authors proposed the theory that people in incestuous families have long and painful experiences with deprivation and separation. As a consequence, family members who are attempting to cope with intense fears of abandonment become less concerned with community standards and mores and more invested in obtaining even a minimal amount of nurturance. Incest seemed to serve the function of keeping the family together at all cost, according to the authors, and the entire family, including nonparticipant members, are involved in supporting and condoning the incestuous activity. The goal of incest then is to keep the family together, to reduce fears and anxiety, to address the sexual estrangement of the parents, and to have all the needs of the family and family members met internally.

Denial to Reality

During the '60s, an acceptance that incest was occurring in families of all strata and socioeconomic groups, helped to present a more realistic picture of incest and introduced the possibility that incest vastly exceeded reported figures (Cormier, 1962; Summit, Roland, and Kryso, 1978). Additionally, researchers were beginning to formulate studies that were designed to assess the prevalence of childhood sexual abuse and its effects upon the victims. However, the issue of denial has been a strong one to overcome and even today when incest is acknowledged to have occurred, the therapeutic focus typically revolves around the girl's desire for her father, her initiation of the act, her seduction of him and others, her pleasure, gratification, and gain (Brickman, 1984).

The influence of Freud and his Oedipal theory are clearly demonstrated when this approach is taken. Although some progress has been made in acknowledging the existence of the problem of incest and placing the responsibility clearly where it belongs, to the perpetrator and not the victim, Freud's retraction of his original statement that incest was a reality in the lives of his patients has blinded many practitioners to the incest that is all around them (O'Hare and Taylor, 1933). Statements by authors such as Foster (1988), who believe that children do not fantasize about sexual activity, is a major and important breakthrough for victims and should bode well for their being taken seriously and treated appropriately.

Sex vs. Power

Incest is oftentimes characterized as a sexual issue. This leads to an inaccurate view of the problem and takes the focus off the fact that incest is a power disorder. Sgroi (1983) states that this power-sex misconception interferes with the ability of professionals to concentrate upon the appropriate issues and to provide the most effective intervention. Shapiro (1987) further states that the description of incest as sexual, and not the misuse of power, may lead the abused child to feel that she has caused the sexual activity to occur, and, therefore, to feel responsible for the abusive behavior. In her study on self-blame and self-mutilation, Shapiro attempted to discover the connection, if any, between the occurrence of incest and subsequent self-mutilating behavior by the victims and found that the acts of self-mutilation suggest more than a causal association with incest.

The Scope of the Problem

Several studies have demonstrated that approximately one female in four is sexually molested during childhood or adolescence (Finkelhor, 1979; Herman, 1983; Rush, 1980). Russell offers a statistic that comes from the first large-scale probability household sample she completed in 1986. When two categories of childhood sexual abuse were combined (incestuous and extrafamilial), 38% (357) of the 930 women polled reported at least one experience of sexual victimization before reaching the age of eighteen; 28% (258) reported at least one such experience before reaching the age of fourteen (Russell, 1986). Finkelhor (1979), it should be noted, estimated that the figure for male sexual abuse is one out of ten boys under the age of eleven.

Offenders, according to Foster (1988) are 98% male and include brothers, grandfathers, uncles, fathers or father surrogates. It is estimated that 90% of victims are females, but male victimization is believed to be underreported according to Foster and Finkelhor (1979). Foster further states that reports of 16 percent of adult females who claim to have been victims of intrafamilial sexual abuse indicate that it occurs more commonly than peptic ulcer disease or diabetes. Those who view incest from a feminist perspective (Herman, 1977, 1983; Russell, 1988) tend to take into account power issues, the offender as male and responsible for his behavior, and an acknowledgment that the patriarchy inherent in any culture predisposes the male to misuse power within his family and society. The feminist model describes incestuous activity as occurring between an active, resistant but powerless victim and powerful, intrusive, self-serving offender (Brickman, 1984). It will not be possible, according to Brickman, to "prevent" incest without eradicating the traditional dominant-submissive sexual power structure which serves an important social function of keeping women in their place.

The consequences of incest/childhood sexual abuse are long-lasting and intense, as reported by numerous clinicians (Courtois, 1988; Herman, 1977, 1983; Rush, 1980). Victims report that they have difficulty forming trusting relationships with both men and women. They oftentimes abuse alcohol or other substance, suffer depression, sexual dysfunction, and low self-esteem. Sexual abuse victims have difficulty being self-assertive, have repeated victimizations, and have a high incidence of suicide attempts (Cole, 1982).

Clinicians and researchers have recently begun to liken the effects of incest to that of post-traumatic stress syndrome and suggest that an adult victim's response to the incest trauma can be viewed as chronic traumatic neurosis resulting in repression and dissociative numbing to stimuli associated with the original abuse (Courtois, 1988; Gelinas, 1983). Such numbing, it appears, is never totally effective, and repeated intrusions occur often in the form of vivid flashbacks that create a heightened sense of vulnerability and a desire to seek treatment (Johnson, 1989).

Treatment, however, is usually sought for peripheral issues such as relationship problems, and the incest is not disclosed to the therapist (Gelinas,1983; Westermeyer,1978). Consequently, when victims enter therapy with a "disguised presentation" as described by Gelinas, and the incest history remains hidden, its negative effects are not available for treatment. Victims, under these circumstances, remain untreated and clinicians are not able to advance their knowledge of the problem and enhance their skills in treating sexual abuse victims (Faria and Belohlavek, 1984). Conversely, as women begin to share their incest experiences and the results of the treatment in which they have participated and, hopefully, benefited, theoreticians and clinicians will have more information and data on which to build their treatment modalities and to formulate strategies for change. Knowledge of symptoms and pathology of those in treatment has been documented and has been necessary for appropriate treatment interventions and strategies to be provided. However, information about the strengths, appropriate coping mechanisms, and resources of adult survivors is important both for an accurate understanding of the effects of sexual abuse and for the clinicians responsible for providing treatment to have an accurate and more complete picture of the client.

Lowenthal and Chiriboga (1973) contend that learning more about resources of an individual will allow researchers to delineate more comprehensive models of coping and understand how people adapt to particular stages in their lives. Most studies thus far have sought to delineate the deficits and the dysfunction of the adult survivor of childhood sexual abuse (Gold, 1986; Feinauer, 1988). Attempts have been made to show a significant difference in levels of self-esteem, depression, and sexual dysfunction, among others, between victims and non-vicitms of childhood sexual abuse. The importance of this focus cannot be minimized as it is necessary to understand the problem of incest and its consequences in order to provide appropriate treatment. What has not been sufficiently dealt with to this point are the strength and coping resources that survivors of sexual abuse have developed as a result of having survived their experiences (Bass and Davis, 1988). Survivors seek therapy, in many instances, because much of their energy is drained by the past that continues to haunt them, but their ability to survive points to the enormous strengths they possess (Goodman and Nowak-Scibelli, 1985). As with anyone seeking treatment, the incest victim is encouraged to contribute her own coping skills, personality, ego strengths, and defense mechanisms to the process (Faria and Belohlavek, 1984; Menaghan, 1983).

Bass and Davis, in their book *The Courage to Heal* describe a number of coping mechanisms that survivors of childhood sexual abuse have used in an attempt to deal with their victimization. The authors also provide a great deal of information, guidance, and resources to help the adult survivor begin the process of healing. It is a book that has helped women to break through their isolation by illustrating how other victims have worked through their pain and trauma.

This brief outline of how incest has evolved historically is necessary for a more complete understanding of the problem. For the purposes of this book, *How to Claim Your Power*, it places the issue of power in a perspective that can now be better understood by the reader. From denial to acceptance that incest is a reality, we are beginning to deal with the ramifications of sexual abuse and take responsibility for its treatment and prevention. Understanding is important, particularly for those who treat adult survivors. It tells us where we have been and oftentimes points out where we need to go. We are now ready to claim our power.

QUESTIONNAIRE

Step 3 Learn where you became stuck.

If you were sexually abused as a child, at what age (or approximate) were you abused?

Note the following chart with age-appropriate behaviors and the stage or stages you were in when abused. Check those behaviors or activities that apply to you. This will help you to learn where and why you are stuck in your life now. You may have no clear memory of how old you were when abused. This is not unusual nor does it pose an insurmountable obstacle to your healing process. You can still use these stages as a way to learn when you were victimized or stuck as a result.

Age 2–3

- Child doesn't like to share.
- Strong urges and desires. Child developing self-control and sometimes can solve problems before acting.
- Tries to please parents or caretakers but often cannot control impulses.
- Openly affectionate, especially with parents or caretakers.
- Able to entertain oneself.
- Can communicate with others. Child becoming very verbal. Enjoys talking to herself.

- Beginning to develop an interest in other children.
- Child enjoys fantasy and loves to imitate other people.
- Child can engage in creative activities.

Age 3–4

- Child sees herself as part of a family. She knows her name, sex, and age.
- Sharing her things is difficult for the child to do.
- Interacts with other children and is able to play well with them..
- Enjoys growing up and learning how to master new skills.
- Child is able to do very simple household chores.
- Child is very curious and asks "Why" often, wants to know the purpose for everything.
- Fantasy life is still important to the child. She continues to enjoy imitating other people.
- Child's cognitive development has progressed to drawing recognizable objects, understanding some number concepts, knowing her colors, and beginning to become interested in letters of the alphabet.
- Child is now able to converse more effectively and is beginning to reason things out.

Age 4–6

- Child is beginning to play more cooperatively with others; begins to develop the willingness to take turns and to share.
- Increased attention span is present. Language is becoming more complex. Child can express ideas, participate in discussions, ask questions.
- Child displays independence; begins to protect herself and can advocate for her rights.
- Identifies with parents or caretakers and tries to imitate them.
- Child selects "best friends."
- Child is aware of how others view her and is able to change her image of self based on the opinions of others.

Age 6–12

- Child is developing a unique personality. Peer and group identification is very important; judges herself increasingly by the attitudes and beliefs of peers.
- Same-sex interaction and play more often than not the rule.

- Strong sense of fairness begins to develop.
- Social interaction very important but child can entertain herself if necessary.
- School success becomes increasingly more important and the means by which the child measures her worth.
- Child begins to use language with some degree of creativity and can tell jokes.
- Child experiences some discomfort with the conflict between her parents' belief system and those of her peer age group.
- Rules are becoming very important and knowledge increases about the need to follow these rules.
- Craves attention from adults.
- An increased sense of responsibility is developing for the care of oneself and even of younger siblings.
- Independence is increasing, but the young girl is still dependent emotionally on the adults in her life and looks to them for help and support.

Age 12–18/Adolescence

- Adolescent needs a great deal of help in adjusting to changes that are occurring so that youngster can maintain a strong personal sense of values and identity.
- Adolescent has extreme mood swings but often doesn't know how to express anger.
- More social with a need to be independent of parents and to rely more on peers; develops strong emotional attachments and involvements.
- Able to introspect and has a strong sense of how things are and how they should be; developing a personal code of morality.
- Behavior continues to be determined by peer group.
- Adolescent begins to give some thought to vocation and holds a part-time job in order to make her own money.
- Some adolescents show an interest in school and their future,while others lose interest in school and neglect their studies.
- Rebelliousness from the norms of society and the parental system may create a great deal of tension between parents and he adolescent; adoption of extreme ways of dressing and hair style, destructive behavior. Individualization is a common theme.
- Emotional attachments outside the family are formed with less reliance on the family for affection and support.

The Many
Faces of Power

4

Power, n. 1. ability to do or act; capability of doing or accomplishing something. 2. political or national strength. 3. great or marked ability to do or act; strength; might; force. 4. the possession of control or command over others; authority; ascendancy.

—The Random House College Dictionary

In her book *Toward a New Psychology of Women*, Jean Baker Miller writes: "'Power' is almost a dirty word—in somewhat the same way 'sex' has been. For women especially it has been an unmentionable subject." If we think of power as the ability to accomplish something, to exhibit strength, to act according to what is in one's best interest or in the best interest of others, then power can be seen as something positive. Power in and of itself is not destructive or a malevolent force. It is not something to be feared or avoided. Power is energy, pure and simple, and it can be used for good or evil, but without power, nothing can be accomplished.

Try getting out of bed in the morning without the power to swing your legs over the side. Try walking or running or speaking or writing or doing anything without power and energy. Power is the fuel that makes everything happen in your life. Obviously power can be used in negative and destructive ways. There is evidence of the misuse of power all around us. Women who have been victims of childhood sexual abuse know all too well how power is misused and of how powerless people can be victimized by others. Child victims become victims because they have no power and sadly lack powerful people in their lives who can use their power to advocate for them. Power is not something to be avoided, but something that has to be nurtured, reinforced, and used in ways that are constructive and positive.

What are the faces of power?

Confrontation is power; love is power; anger is power; money is power; silence is power; communication is power; education is power; honesty is power; hope is power; giving up is power; holding on is power; contentment with what you have is power; aspiring to be more and do more is power; forgiving is power; withholding forgiveness is power; and on and on . . .

Power cannot be avoided. The only question is who has it and how is it being used. If you are powerless, unable to make things happen or keep them from happening, then you will likely be vulnerable to further victimization. What we have learned about the cycle of victimization is that people who have been victimized tend to repeat the cycle and victimize others who are less powerful than themselves. While the reasons for this may be difficult to understand, what we have learned is that the cycle can be broken. The women in this book illustrate that fact very clearly. The misuse of power is something that victims learn. The appropriate use of power is something that survivors can know if they stop viewing power in a negative way and see it as a means to be productive, constructive, and an ally instead of the enemy.

This book is about power. It's about power and adult survivors of childhood sexual abuse who have been victims of the misuse of power. As a survivor and a therapist who has worked over the years with many women who have struggled to overcome the consequences of abuse, I have learned a great deal about power. I have realized that in order to be a survivor in every sense of the word, one must feel powerful and in control of her life.

Power is not something readily available to women in our society. One has only to look at the images of power that are part of the media and popular press—Rocky, Arnold Schwarzenegger, Saddam Hussein, and the Incredible Hulk,—for example, to know that this is true. Every once in a while a powerful woman emerges such as Margaret Thatcher, Gloria Steinem, Barbara Walters, or Helen Gurley Brown, but for the most part, power belongs to the male gender, and there are few opportunities for women to study other powerful women in order to learn how to be powerful themselves.

In fact, because women are all too often the victims of more powerful people—parents, husbands, employers—the opposite is usually the case. Women learn how to be powerless and find that their powerlessness is rewarded and reinforced. In working with women who have been victimized, or even with women who were not overtly victimized, I have seen many instances in which women have had great difficulty becoming empowered. The reasons women remain in a powerless position, unable to tap into their reservoirs of strength and power, are numerous and complex. Suffice it to say that women have been limited in the ways they can be powerful and use that power in their lives.

We begin by looking at three instances which illustrate how women view power. There are circumstances and situations unique to each individual that determine whether or not she can or will choose to be powerful. All three of these illustrations, however, reveal how women try to avoid claiming their power. They show that power is often viewed as negative and counterproductive and not something that will enhance a person's life and help her to avoid further victimization. All of the women began in a less powerful position than they needed to be to change their lives. Most of the women eventually claimed their power which dramatically affected their lives. One did not. We can learn from both.

The Power of Beauty

I remember vividly a woman I saw in my counseling practice. She was an attractive, middle-aged woman who came for her first appointment impeccably dressed. Based on her appearance alone, she made a very favorable first impression, which I'm sure was no accident. I learned quickly that she relied a great deal upon her personal appearance and her considerable attractiveness to gain many things she wanted and needed in life.

Anne shared with me that she was very concerned by the fact that as each year passed, she became more and more worried how she was going to sustain her quite stunning appearance so she could continue to get all the "goodies" that came with being a beautiful woman in our society. She told me that all her life she had been able to use her looks to succeed, or at least to gain an advantage over those who were not blessed with attractiveness. She had learned very early in life that there was a "power" that came with being beautiful, one which she willingly used and was loathe to relinquish.

In fact, although possessing a flawless complexion which was virtually wrinkle free, Anne was thinking seriously about having a face-lift to tighten her skin and give her what she hoped would be a more youthful appearance. She came to me to get a second opinion about the wisdom of this decision and also to ask whether or not I could see the difference as she gently pulled the skin of her face back.

I could see a slight difference, but that difference didn't significantly change her appearance. She really was quite lovely and very young looking for her age. I told her as much, but she only seemed grateful to hear that at least some improvement could be made in her appearance, however small.

One of the most important requisites of a therapist is to be non-judgmental, so I was not about to tell Anne that I thought she was wrong to spend a ton of money on plastic surgery, at least at this time. Who was I to say what was right or wrong for this woman? If it made her feel more secure, better about herself, then perhaps a face-lift could be therapeutic for her.

However, what I could do was get her to focus on how she could feel attractive and secure and powerful by appreciating and using other parts of herself. I believed that I could help Anne to find a source of power that wouldn't fade with the advancing years but instead would grow and become stronger. I could work with her to develop an internal sense of worth and competence that didn't depend exclusively on her looks. The prospect was exciting.

So I didn't try to dissuade Anne from her goal of improving what didn't need much improvement. What I did do was suggest that she and I could work on helping her to feel empowered as a woman in a different way. The moment I mentioned the word "power" to Anne, it was as if I had thrown a bucket of cold water on her.

"Oh, I don't want to be powerful," she responded emphatically. My first thought was that we needed to agree on the definition of power, and that perhaps I had been too hasty in just tossing out a word that I knew oftentimes had a negative connotation for women.

"Anne," I said, "I'm talking about power as energy. I'm talking about something that everyone needs if she is to feel safe in this world and in control of her life as much as she can be. I'm talking about something that is not dependent upon youth or attractiveness or a perfect body."

Anne listened politely, but I sensed that she was not buying any of it. I tried once more. "Anne, I'm not saying that to be attractive is wrong. I love looking good and having people think I'm attractive. I'm fully aware that attractive people, like it or not, have a leg up in the world. I'm for anything that gives someone an advantage while not taking anything from someone else. What I'm asking you to do is consider what I'm saying and work with me to develop another kind of power. I'm talking about doing this while you improve your appearance as well. They are not mutually exclusive activities. And think what you would gain if you had both—beauty and power."

Anne agreed to think about what I had proposed, but I had the distinct feeling that I had been speaking a foreign language to her, one that she either would not or could not hear and understand. She made a second appointment, canceled it the following week, and I never saw her again.

There are many reasons why Anne, and indeed many other women, either can't or won't make the choice to be powerful. One would think that having been on the losing end of the power game a number of times, a woman would work diligently to learn how to come out on the winning end. But that's not always the case; unfortunately, it seems to work the other way. Perhaps it goes back to doing what feels familiar or right. Or it could be that to gain power, one must have a certain amount of it in order to go forward. It's almost like priming the pump. There's a saying: "It takes money to make money." Maybe "it takes power to make power."

The Power of Relationships

One of the obstacles to our claiming our power and acting upon it is that oftentimes when we are powerful, even appropriately powerful, those people with whom we have relationships, either personally or professionally, may feel threatened. There is even a chance that we may jeopardize or even lose these relationships. For women this is a particularly difficult problem. We are the ones who are supposed to build and nurture relationships. We are the ones who are expected to sacrifice in order to maintain relationships. We are the ones who try to avoid doing anything that might create a breech in our relationships.

Men are expected to be powerful. Women are expected to maintain stability. For a woman to act in a powerful way and change the rules of the game can cause conflict in relationships. As a result women internalize the message that overt power is to be avoided and, therefore, make the hard choice to suppress their power in order to maintain harmony in their relationships. Sometimes the cost is very dear.

For instance, how many of us still tolerate abusive behavior either within or outside of our families? We hold onto this belief that others have more power than we do and that they can use that power to do whatever they choose to in their relationships with us. In the face of repeated victimizations, subtle and not so subtle, we react as victims. We become powerless, immobilized. But the worst part of this continual cycle of immobility is that we come to believe that there's nothing we can do. We know that it will always be this way, so we feel we have no choice but to try and outlast the situation. After all, we know that we can't ever do anything to change things. That's just the way they are.

The next story is about a woman who was in actuality a powerful, resourceful person, but who had buried her power so deeply and so well that it took a great deal of effort on her part to find it and use it personally and professionally.

I've worked with a number of women who come from the "that's just the way things are" school of thought. Theresa was one of those women when she came to me for counseling. I knew of Theresa because she operated one of the most successful small businesses in town. Her father had started the heating oil company some years before, after the depression, and Theresa had taken over the running of the business as her father became older. The long-range plan was that Theresa would one day own the business when her father retired. Theresa was known and respected in town as a very astute and competent businesswoman, and the company was thriving under her capable leadership.

Theresa had come a long way since her marriage and her subsequent divorce from Artie. Artie had been, according to Theresa, physically and verbally abusive throughout their marriage. Theresa had been his victim for many years and had learned well the lessons of victimization. After their very difficult divorce, made even more difficult for Theresa by virtue of the fact that she was still a victim, Theresa began to gradually become stronger and professionally at least, more powerful. However, the power Theresa was experiencing seemed always to be external to who and what she was. She could own the fact that she had an excellent business sense, that her employees respected her and worked hard for her, that she was continuing to build the business her father had started, but Theresa always saw these qualities as what she did, not who she was. This fact was graphically illustrated by the fact that after their divorce, Artie continued to work for the fuel company with the support of Theresa's father, who still thought of Artie as his son-in-law. Some habits die hard—we all know that.

Artie continued to verbally abuse Theresa every chance he got and used his status as "the ex" to gain special privileges at work. Needless to say, this undermined Theresa greatly although most of the employees sympathized with her predicament and knew that Artie was still with the company because of "the old man." This situation continued to eat away at Theresa and intensified as she gradually began to shed her role as victim. Theresa remarried, and her second husband was a man who neither needed nor required her to be a victim, so she was able to develop into a strong and capable woman.

But Theresa was still stuck. She was stuck because she could not feel a sense of internal, personal power, the power that she needed in order to confront her father about Artie and then give Artie his walking papers.

I was struck by how inappropriate it was for Artie even to be working for Theresa. Under the best of circumstances, this would have been a very difficult relationship to manage: an ex-wife the boss of her ex-husband. Talk about your challenges. And in this particular situation, the ex-husband (who, I was told, to add fuel to the fire, was an active alcoholic), was verbally abusive and constantly tried to intimidate his ex-wife. In the meantime "the old man" treated Artie as if he was still part of the family, and Theresa had the added problem of having to ask her father to give up that relationship and allow her to fire Artie.

It all seemed very clear-cut to me. Theresa was still Artie's victim, and she didn't need to be. In fact, until she broke away from that abusive relationship completely and took control of the situation, no matter how successful she became, she would still be a victim. Theresa knew all of this, she had known it for years, but knowing it and being able to act upon it were two different things. She came to me to get some help and to find a way to stand up to both of these "powerful" men in her life.

First of all, Theresa was terrified of confronting her father. She was certain that in doing so she would lose not only the battle but also his love and, ultimately, she might lose her position in the company, a company her father still technically owned. These were rather big losses to contemplate: her father and her livelihood. Obviously one doesn't make a reckless or hasty decision when so much is at stake.

However, I felt that it was my responsibility to point out to Theresa what she would lose by not making the powerful moves necessary to rid herself of Artie's continued victimization. I told her that she would never, could never, be truly powerful either personally or professionally while she endured this situation. She might only be able to cower in the face of abuse or endure pain, humiliation and injustice instead of learning to walk away from it or confront it. I told Theresa that no loss was worth that. If her father rejected her because she refused to be a victim, then she had to accept that and deal with it.

Incidentally, I pointed out to Theresa that should her father choose to lose her rather than allow her to take a stand against Artie, he would probably suffer the greater loss. After all, Theresa had always been a very loving and considerate daughter. Also, by taking over the reins of the business, a business that her father was now able to phase in and out of at his own discretion until he could accept retirement, she had been able to relieve him of a tremendous burden.

It was also clear that Theresa could always get a job, particularly since she had earned the admiration and respect of the people in the community for the fine job she was doing at the fuel company. All of these were factors that needed to be taken into consideration and certainly added some weight to the scale in Theresa's favor. The mentality of the victim, however, sometimes does not allow her to see or feel the possibility of her power, to appreciate her resources and to believe that those resources will carry her through a difficult situation. This was true for Theresa. All the marvelous things that she had accomplished, beginning with finding the courage and the strength to walk out of an abusive relationship, were all clouded over by the overwhelming belief that others were in control of her life. Theresa was immobilized and would remain immobilized until she could feel powerful enough and secure enough in that power to undertake the changes she needed to make. I was determined to help her do that.

We began with the "power of the plan." Every good solution needs a good plan, so we set a goal and started working toward it. My job as we began to move forward was to constantly encourage and support Theresa. I needed to remind her each time we met that she was truly a powerful woman. I reflected back to her all the things she had done in her life that proved it. She was running a small business very successfully; she had divorced an abusive man; she had raised two lovely daughters as a single parent, she had recently remarried a strong and caring man. Theresa needed to recognize and claim her power if she was to deal with these two men, her father and Artie, whom she believed had all the power over her life while she had none.

The plan was to talk to her father, explain the impossibility of her working with Artie any longer, tell her father that she planned to dismiss Artie, and then do it. Theresa was weak-kneed scared and put off the confrontation a couple of times, but she finally found the courage and power to speak to her father. He listened, he reacted very little, and he agreed that if that's what she wanted to do, it was okay with him. All Theresa's fears about her father rejecting her in favor of Artie had been just that: fears with no foundation. All her father asked was to remain separate and apart from Artie's dismissal; obviously he wanted to avoid any negative reaction from Artie.

Theresa was elated. Her father hadn't rejected her; he supported her. She now felt powerful enough for the next stage of the plan, which was to fire Artie.

Theresa told Artie he was no longer needed at the company. Artie protested, but Theresa stood her ground. He threatened to sue Theresa, claiming that he had a contract for hauling oil, but his threats proved to be about as empty as any real power that Theresa had imagined he had had over her all these years. Theresa learned that it was she who really had the power, that she had always had the power. She had just needed to find it and use it.

Since that time, Theresa has continued to tap into her power source to accomplish other things in her life. It hasn't always been easy. Casting aside many years of behaving a certain way or believing certain things about yourself is difficult. It's almost like reshaping the mold in order to create a new person. In Theresa's case, she discovered her power, the power she had surrendered when she had become Artie's victim. Then she had to reclaim that power and use it in her life. It was wonderful to watch that process take place in Theresa's life and then to continue watching her grow and develop.

Theresa worked long and hard to no longer be a victim, not Artie's victim nor anyone else's. She had to confront her fear and her insecurity; she had to test her limits and risk some losses. Theresa ultimately had to believe that she had the power to make important changes and to accept the consequences. For Theresa the outcome was positive. She was freed from Artie's abuse and freed from the fear that her father would rather lose her than support her. But, most importantly, Theresa was freed from whatever force had held her captive for so long. Her fear, that by advocating powerfully for herself she would lose the relationship she had with her only living parent, proved to be wrong. Theresa could be powerful and maintain a relationship at the same time. She did not have to give up one in order to claim the other. Theresa claimed her power, and when she did, she claimed her life.

It is no exaggeration, I believe, to say that in claiming our power, like Theresa, we claim our life. When we allow forces outside ourselves to control us, to dictate our behaviors and our feelings, to determine what course our lives will take, we have no life, not really. We exist at the whim of people like Artie, or people who take and don't give, or people who would have us be victims so they can feel powerful. We are swallowed up in the world of other people's actions and can only react to what they say or do. We become like ghosts with a form but no substance.

But once we fill ourselves with the power of our own choices or needs, we become fleshed out and filled in. We become stronger and more in control of what happens to us and when. And isn't that what makes life so meaningful and special? Theresa found that out. She put aside her fears, but most of all, she put aside her role as victim. Instead of Theresa saying, "That's just the way it is," when faced with a negative situation now, she thinks about how it can be or should be . . . and she makes it happen.

The Power of the Group

A couple of years ago, I accompanied my husband to Israel on a three-month sabbatical from the ministry. I had hoped while I was there to do some volunteer work with a women's organization which I thought would be able to utilize my skills as someone who worked with victimized women. I was directed to a Rape Crisis Center and found that they needed some instruction on how to run support groups for their clients. That was something I believed I could do so I made a presentation to the volunteers in which I said something about the way the group process worked and how groups can be effective vehicles for treatment and support.

The volunteer group seemed interested in having me work with them, but I found out very quickly that there was another agenda troubling the volunteers that needed to be addressed. It seems that this Rape Crisis Center, which had been established about a decade before, had two distinct groups of volunteers: the vanguard that had started the center and wanted things to remain status quo, and the newer volunteers who were interested in the structure of the center and the way it was going to build for the future.

The two groups appeared to be at odds a good deal of the time, and the newer volunteers, with whom I was meeting, wanted to either resolve the conflicts or leave. This was a difficult situation because the newer and younger volunteers were committed to their work with victimized women and did not want to abandon either them or their commitment.

I suggested that we could accomplish two tasks at the same time. We could form a group to address the issue of the structure of the center and the conflicts that kept bubbling up, and reflect each week on how the group worked. In that way the volunteers would learn how to lead and participate in a group. This idea appealed to the women, and we agreed to begin the following week.

The women were enthusiastic and eagerly engaged in the group process once we began. We talked about how center staff meetings were particularly frustrating because they seemed more often than not to disintegrate into chaos. Also personal issues got in the way as invariably one woman's style was not compatible with another's, and the meetings would sometimes be focused on whatever issue brought this to the fore. The bottom line was that not much productive work was accomplished, and the women ended up feeling that they were wasting their time, which for busy people is a precious commodity.

My first question was: "Why isn't there an agenda for these meetings? How can anything be accomplished if no one knows and is prepared for the business that will come up and if there is no structure for the meeting?" Nobody seemed to know the answer except to say, "That's the way it's always been done." I had difficulty understanding how such a group of intelligent women, women who were dedicated to making a very real difference in their society, could end up spinning their wheels instead of focusing their energy on making positive changes. I filed that question away for future reference.

The second week that the group met I began by asking who would like to lead the group that week. I was met with silence. "Come on, ladies," I said. "You're all, each and every one of you, capable of running this group." Still nobody volunteered to chair the meeting. "Look," I said, "I can lead this group every week if you want me to, but you're not going to learn as much by watching me as you will if you do it yourself."

Sharon, one of the braver members of the group, slowly raised her hand. She agreed to give it a try even though she "knew" that she probably wouldn't do very well. I wondered where this lack of confidence, obviously shared by each of the eight women present, had come from. I had no doubt from the little I knew of Sharon that she would do a commendable job, but I kept that feeling to myself, not wanting to set her up to meet some expectation that I had of her.

Of course, Sharon did a great job of facilitating the meeting. When it was over, and it was time for us to process what we had learned about how to run a group, I told her so. By that time Sharon had begun to realize that I did not possess some magic or remarkable quality that made it possible for me to lead a group while no one else could. In fact Sharon knew that she had done a very good job of listening, reflecting, and directing and redirecting the group, and that it had been a very productive meeting. She teased me about being a hopeless cheerleader. She was certainly right about that, but I had been right about her having what it took to do the job.

When I asked for a volunteer the following week, a number of women were eager to try what Sharon had succeeded in doing, and from then on, I was able to sit back somewhat and watch the other women take the reins and lead the group. I was still rather dismayed by the lack of confidence that I sensed from these women, however. They were bright, thoughtful, and successful in the work they did outside the center, but they never seemed able to channel their energies appropriately or to direct their power for their own good and the good of their clients while working at the center.

It wasn't as if they were working in an organization in which men were in power and control, and they had little choice but to remain in the submissive role. The center was staffed entirely by women. They all appeared to share the common goal of helping victimized women heal and get on with their lives. However, they seemed diffused, poorly focused, not in charge of their individual resources and not in control of what was happening within the center. I could see that they were not using their power appropriately or effectively and wondered why this was happening throughout the entire system at the center, from the older all the way down to the newer volunteers. I shared with the group that I thought in some ways they had joined their client population through their inability to get unstuck and become mobilized. This was a rather strong statement to make, but by the time I said it I knew that our group was cohesive and would not be terribly threatened by what one person perceived to be the truth.

My comment prompted a discussion about whether or not this could indeed be an accurate observation and, if so, why it was that way and what could be done about it. The group agreed that if they were really stuck in their own dysfunctional system without the ability to create positive and necessary changes, then how could they model a different way of dealing with problems to their clients?

As a result of this discussion, the group shared with me their belief that they could be powerful as individuals and as a group. They had just about everything it takes to do that. When they began to analyze why solutions to problems at the center never emerged, they looked to the larger state system for their answer. They started to gain some insight into how they participated as women in the state of Israel. Israel, they recognized, was a country surrounded by danger. While secure for the most part, the fact of the matter was that at any given moment, the country might be under siege from any number of people located very close to their borders. The army, which was comprised of some women but not women who were expected to engage in combat, was an army of men. Israel was dependent upon its men for safety and security. The people of Israel, therefore, had to support and encourage its male population.

Israel was also a country that had an ethos that men have their place, which is traditionally in positions of power and control, and women have their place, which is not in positions of power and control. Of course there have been, and continue to be, exceptions to this rule, but for the most part, Israel adhered to the old system of supporting male superiority in order to invest their army with the confidence and strength they needed to defend the country.

Now, granted this analysis came out of a lot of theorizing that could be rejected as idle discussion, but it seemed to work as a way to explain why the women of the center "participated," even unknowingly, in a type of collusion. After all, survival and the desire to survive supersede all other concerns, and these competent women could be repressing their personal power in order to be part of the overall "plan" to help the men feel and be powerful.

So what was the outcome? We decided to accept that premise and to acknowledge that by owning and using their power to effect positive changes in the center and in society, the women would not be undermining the men in Israel. In fact, if the women could become appropriately powerful, it would ease the burden for everyone, since they would be able to function more effectively for their own good and the good of the country, if necessary.

The first step was to take some action within the center. We decided to tackle the issue of the chaotic, unstructured and disorganized staff meetings. One of the women volunteered to speak to the older group of volunteers and offer to facilitate the next staff meeting. Yehudit was a bright and very well-organized woman who hoped to bring these qualities to the larger group and see whether or not it was possible to solve this particular frustrating problem.

Yehudit was given permission to chair the next meeting, and she immediately drew up an agenda, requesting input from the other members of the staff. The agenda was posted. The meeting's starting and ending times were noted so everyone would know the amount of time allotted to complete their business. Because of the agenda, the volunteers were aware of the issues that would be brought up and, therefore, could prepare themselves to offer valuable information.

As it turned out, my stay in Israel was over before I could hear about the results of this experiment. However, I did receive a very enthusiastic letter from a member of the group, who shared with me that the staff meeting had gone beautifully and that a lot had been accomplished. It had also adjourned five minutes early with its business completed, which had never happened before. The group was immediately reinforced by their powerful move of changing the structure of the meeting, and decided that they could be strong and powerful and make important changes without threatening the social order of the center and of their country.

I also heard that the group had decided to continue meeting after my departure. I was very pleased that our work together had stimulated some necessary changes for these women and that they had gotten in touch with their power and had gained some sense of why they had probably repressed it in the past. I can't help but wonder whether or not these women would have found their power or even searched for it had we not tackled this issue as a group and come up with a possible explanation for their "selective powerlessness."

I realized through this experience with the women of the center that there are more reasons than being victimized as a child that block women from owning their power. Perhaps for every individual woman and each group of women there is a certain, unique reason for taking or rejecting power. Women do share a response to what society dictates as acceptable or unacceptable behavior, power being one attribute that is "supposed" to belong to men, but beyond that, there seem to be many difficult factors which might influence them. All I know is that we have to start asking questions if we are to come up with answers and finally be able to claim our power. The women of the center surely did that, and I have heard since that they have continued to make powerful moves in their lives and to develop the power we tapped into within the group.

My education about the dynamic of power was certainly broadened by my work at the Rape Crisis Center in Israel, and I was able to bring some of what I learned into my group work at home. In fact I decided to begin an empowerment group for a small group of women who were stuck in much the same way as my friends in Israel. We met intensely for six weeks and were able to accomplish a number of powerful moves in our lives with the insight and help of the group. I began as I did with the women of the center by identifying the ways in which we were powerless and stuck in that powerlessness. From there we found ways to help one another and to find our power both as individuals and as a group. It worked in Israel, and it worked for us.

QUESTIONNAIRE

Step 4 Learn who and what has the power in your life.

The power over you:

1. Who has the power? _____

2. What has the power? _____

3. How did this happen? _____

4. Is this power constructive? _____ destructive? _____

5. Do you want to change this situation? _____

6. Do you know how to change this situation? _____

7. In what context do you usually become "the victim"?

       _____ relationships

       _____ work   _____ school

       _____ family   _____ all of the above

8. Have you ever been a powerful person?

When? _____

Why? _____

_____

_____

9. What patterns of power or powerlessness do you see repeated in your life? _____

_____

10. What powerful person can you use as an example of someone who could change the situation? What characteristics does this person have? _____

_____

When you have claimed your power, note how this happened and what effect it had on your life.

The Power
Within

5

> *I have met brave women who are exploring the outer edge of human possibility with no history to guide them, and with a courage to make themselves vulnerable that I find moving beyond the words to express it.*
> —*Gloria Steinem,* Outrageous Acts and Everyday Rebellions

How we came to learn about power, the messages that we got about where it comes from, who has it and who hasn't were very critical lessons for us. Those of us who were sexually abused as children learned that power came from outside of us and that we had no power to control our abuse or stop it. Any sense of personal power that we might have been able to develop, that indeed we should have developed, was blocked, suppressed, negated.

From then on we knew that all we could do in the face of circumstances and events that we had no power over was to respond. Our lives have been spent responding to situations. We react instead of act. That leaves us powerless to determine much of what happens in our lives. We develop a sense of hopelessness or anger or depression instead of feeling creative, powerful, in charge.

What we need to do, what we have to do now, is recognize that what happened to us as children does not have to determine how we live as surviving adults. That decision requires us to relearn the lessons of personal, internal power and use those lessons to make positive changes in our lives so we can be in control of what happens to us as much as possible.

The women whose stories I am about to tell are women who were all victims of childhood sexual abuse. They grew up learning that power was both destructive and unavailable to them. It took them many years of hard work to heal from the trauma of their victimization and to learn that power is a tool necessary to live as a survivor and not as a victim. They claimed their power in ways that may seem insignificant to those people who have never known the feeling of being powerless, but these are major steps for women who have had to learn from the ground up how to be powerful.

Maggie's Story

One of Maggie's most painful childhood memories is standing in the driveway of her parents' palatial home in the suburbs of Massachusetts and watching her father leave. She didn't realize it at the time, but her father and mother were about to divorce, and she would not see nor hear from her father for many long years.

Maggie was closer to her father than she was to her mother. Her mother was an angry woman, subject to unexpected and violent outbursts. She never missed an opportunity to criticize Maggie in harsh and demeaning ways, and Maggie tried to avoid her as much as possible. Maggie's father, however, although he was a surgeon and did not have a great deal of time to spend with his two daughters, was affectionate and supportive of his children when he was at home. In fact, during the five years of Maggie's brief life, her father had been the only person she had felt accepted her and loved her for who and what she was.

When he left that day, he left an enormous void in Maggie's life. All she had left now in her very narrow world was a bitter woman who was too engrossed in her own pain and frustration to give much of anything to her daughters. That would have been bad enough for a young girl to deal with, but Maggie's life became harsher and more confusing when her mother married Scott, a man who began to sexually abuse Maggie almost from the day he moved into the house.

Scott began by molesting Maggie when he had occasion to be alone with her, and threatened that if she told anyone she would be taken from her family and sent to live with foster parents or even to jail. So Maggie kept this vile secret, and, predictably, the sexual abuse escalated. Now it was accompanied with physical abuse as Scott would fly into a rage when he was abusing Maggie and throw her against the wall or punch her in the stomach. None of the injuries could be seen by other people—abusers are frequently too smart to call attention to what they are doing to their victims—and Maggie maintained her painful silence.

Sometimes Scott would take her down into the cellar where he forced her to perform oral sex. Maggie has terrible memories of this dark and frightening place, a place that remains associated with nightmare visions of physical beatings and forced sexual acts. All this time Maggie lived behind a facade of normalcy, confiding in no one, trusting no one. One time she showed me a picture of herself and her sister that had been taken during the time of her abuse. Maggie had a haunted look to her, almost as if she was screaming on the inside for someone to rescue her from the terrible life she was having to endure from this man who was married to her mother.

One of the many tragedies that was part of this horrible existence for Maggie was that Scott managed, when he was not abusing Maggie, to provide some of the reassurance, acceptance and even affection that she had lost when her father had left. He treated her as if she was special. She needed to feel special; all children need to feel special, so in this respect Maggie was a normal child.

Maggie was torn between telling someone about the abuse and losing the only person who paid any attention to her and enduring the sexual and physical abuse which was part of this father-daughter relationship. Maggie did what many young victims of abuse do: she kept silent and tried to survive as best she could the pain and the anger that she felt about her situation.

Years passed, and the abuse continued. Since Maggie was in boarding school during her high school years, she only had to suffer abuse from Scott when she returned home for vacations and holidays. However, now that Maggie was forming new relationships, many of them were with adults she was beginning to trust and respect, she decided she had to tell someone about her abuse. Maggie hoped and even dared to believe that the person she told would be able to help her escape from her nightmare once and for all.

Maggie finally unburdened herself and told the truth about her life to a gym teacher she had come to know and trust. This teacher knew that regardless of what else happened, Maggie had to tell her mother and hope that her mother would stop this terrible thing from ever happening to her daughter again.

The teacher scheduled a meeting in her office so that Maggie could confront her mother with the truth. When Maggie told her mother about the years of physical and sexual abuse she had suffered at the hands of her stepfather, her mother became incensed. She accused Maggie of lying and told her that she could not return home. Her mother told Maggie that she would make arrangements for her belongings to be delivered to the school and that Maggie would have to make other living arrangements when she was not at school. Scott would remain in the home with Maggie's mother.

Telling her mother about her victimization by Scott had devastating consequences for Maggie. Unfortunately this kind of thing happens more times than not to victims who choose to break the secret and tell of their abuse. While this painful confrontation had forced Maggie's mother to make a choice between her daughter and her husband with Maggie coming out on what seemed to be the losing end, that day Maggie began the long journey from victim to survivor. She had finally said "no" and was now ready to begin the healing process, a process which will likely continue for as long as she lives.

Maggie got help initially through therapy. Not every experience in therapy was a happy or productive one for Maggie, but she persisted. I saw Maggie after a colleague who was moving from the area referred her to me. Maggie had done some very good work with this therapist around the issue of her abuse. Our task was to continue this process and help her become more powerful in her life and make choices that would be the best for her and her well-being. Maggie was having some difficulty with this area since she was still learning how to be an advocate for herself and struggling with the idea that she was worth being treated well, by herself and by others with whom she had relationships.

Maggie was in her mid-twenties by this time and had managed to maintain a somewhat tenuous relationship with her mother. The fact that her mother had abandoned her when she had told of her abuse and had chosen to stay married to her daughter's abuser was painful for Maggie, but victims are used to abandonment and pain. They learn to accept it, to rationalize it, and not to expect better from people who owe them a lot more. They settle for a difficult relationship with a parent and their abuser rather than suffer the pain of having no parental relationship at all.

It was doubly difficult for Maggie to reject the crumbs that her mother offered her because she knew that her mother owed her something, and she wanted to take anything she could get. So when her mother invited her home for the holidays, Maggie went, even though Scott would be there along with so many awful memories.

Maggie struggled with this time after time, but never more than when her mother invited her to spend her vacation with her and Scott in Bermuda. This was a very tempting invitation because the New England winter had been especially cold and long that year. Maggie had been working very hard in her human services job, and she needed the warmth of the Bermuda sun. Maggie's mother agreed to pay for the round-trip flight from Boston and to entertain Maggie in her home, an offer that was almost impossible for Maggie to refuse.

Maggie accepted the offer but not without paying a price. She began to experience terrible anxiety, knowing that she would be staying in the same house with Scott. She had nightmares from which she would awaken in a cold sweat. Visions of her abuse haunted her. All the rage that she had suppressed began to churn in her stomach and pound in her head.

In her therapy sessions Maggie went back and forth between wanting to cancel the trip and wanting and needing a vacation in Bermuda. We debated about how she could get in control of the situation and make this trip a pleasant one, but the solution eluded us.

However, Maggie had worked hard to become powerful in her life, and her efforts were rewarded when she happened upon the answer quite unexpectedly during a conversation with her mother. Ever since the confrontation at school when Maggie had told her mother of her abuse and had been asked to live elsewhere, she and her mother had not spoken of the abuse. Then during this one conversation where Maggie and her mother were talking about Maggie's upcoming trip to Bermuda, Maggie surprised even herself when she told her mother that she would feel very uncomfortable staying in the same house with her abuser. She said that she wanted to make the trip, needed the vacation badly, but was not willing to spend each day being reminded of one of the worst experiences of her childhood. Maggie's mother asked Scott to pick up the other phone and then asked Maggie to tell her stepfather what she had just told her. Maggie courageously and powerfully repeated what she had said and waited for Scott's response.

Scott paused for a moment, obviously quite taken aback by Maggie's honesty and forthrightness. He then offered to leave the house during her visit and stay in a nearby hotel.

It was at this moment that Maggie knew that she had taken control of the situation by admitting how uncomfortable she would feel with Scott in the next bedroom and putting the responsibility for the solution on the source of her discomfort. It felt wonderful, Maggie reported to me, to finally own what was going on with her and say "no" to anything that didn't feel right. Also while powerfully in control of the situation, Maggie was able to make an agreement with Scott.

She said that she would see when she arrived at her mother's home whether or not she felt safe with Scott in the house. If she began to feel anxious or frightened with him close by, she would tell Scott and ask him to leave the house until her vacation was over.

Maggie went to Bermuda shortly thereafter and upon her return home, told me that it had been one of the best vacations she had ever had. She had felt in control of her life and confident that no one would violate her. She also knew that what she had learned would stand her in good stead with other people who came into her life.

Maggie was now truly a survivor and her victimization was losing its awesome control over her and the events in her life. She had advocated for herself and was willing to accept any losses that might come out of the situation in order to live without fear, pain, and the consequences of her abuse. Maggie had finally gained a sense that she was worth fighting for, that her peace of mind and happiness were worth standing up for. She continues to believe that, and she is growing ever stronger and more powerful as she moves forward with her life.

Betty's Story

One day I got a call from a colleague who worked at a local child abuse prevention agency asking me if I would be able to take a client of hers into a group for adult survivors of sexual abuse. She candidly told me that this particular woman had been part of a group she was facilitating and that she was a very difficult woman. She was angry, controlling, and, according to the group facilitator, had been responsible for the group breaking up. I could tell a "hot potato" when I heard about one, but since I had made a commitment to work with a population that had some very serious problems and painful issues, I felt obliged to see this woman.

I knew that I had a way out because it wasn't likely that this woman would have insurance that I could take in my counseling practice. I spoke to this prospective client shortly thereafter and found that indeed she did have an insurance plan restricted to therapists within the system. The only possibility of my being able to see her and be reimbursed by this insurance plan rested on the fact that I had an expertise with adult survivors that might not exist in the system. The prospective client, Betty, agreed to contact her primary physician and find out whether he would agree to refer her to me.

Betty accomplished this minor miracle within days, and although I had initially thought that I would rather be boiled in oil than deal with this woman, I have to admit that I was pretty impressed with her motivation and her ability to get what she needed. We made an appointment to meet to discover where she was in her process of recovery so that I could plug her into whatever therapy she needed, group or individual.

Betty arrived at my office on time and eager to begin yet again with another therapist who might be able to help her deal with her abusive experiences. Betty was open about her life, but by now she had spoken to many therapists, both in and out of hospitals, and it had become second nature to her to reveal where she had been and describe where she wanted to be.

I have heard a lot of stories about women who have been sexually and physically abused, so Betty's story didn't shock me, but in all honesty I have to say that this woman had run the gamut. She had been sexually abused as a very young child by a neighbor, and when her mother had discovered the abuse and brought her to the family doctor, the doctor had minimized the situation and given Betty the message that this sort of thing wasn't very important or hurtful. That had set the stage for Betty to be abused by other people, many other people, the most traumatic and violent having been sexual and physical abuse by her father.

While most young women who suffer sexual abuse by a family member report that physical violence is not part of the incest, Betty's case was the exception. Her father was very abusive physically, threatened Betty emotionally on a regular basis, and violated her sexually for many years until she left the family at the age of seventeen. However, Betty hadn't left until she had taken a knife to her father one night when he had tried to crawl into her bed. Obviously she had decided that she would rather kill or be killed than be sexually victimized any further by this man. The threat to kill her father worked, and he managed to stay away from Betty until she left the home a short time later to live on her own.

Betty's abuse pattern had been well established and reinforced by years of physical and sexual mistreatment, and the pattern continued when she went out on her own. She married a man who eventually sexually abused their own daughter, and as a result Betty lost her daughter to social services and never regained custody again.

These times were very difficult for Betty. She drank alcoholically and attempted suicide more than once. She was hospitalized after the suicide attempts and spent some time in locked wards. Betty reports that while hospitalized, she wasn't helped much in dealing with her abusive past, although her depression and self-destructive behavior were likely the result of her trauma. Betty became a rageful and tough woman, wanting to be better, but not having a clue about getting the help she needed.

Betty was placed on antidepressants and believed that this was the answer for her. Her psychiatrist, although supportive and helpful, did little more than monitor the medication. And so Betty began her search for wellness by following her instincts and putting one foot in front of the other, since that's all she knew how to do.

Betty and I went to work. She remained on her medication, although we talked from time to time about the possibility of her one day being able to cope without antidepressants. It was clear that Betty had a number of things operating in her life that were obstacles to her functioning in a healthier and happier manner. Our job was to help her learn how to become powerful, to make better choices, to believe that she was entitled to a better life.

Some of the more important questions that an adult survivor in treatment must explore with the therapist are: "What do I need in order to heal from my abuse and go forward? What do I need to have happen in my life for me to feel free of the victimization? How do I get to a point where I feel that justice has been done?" Usually I ask these questions of a client early in the process so we both have an idea of what goal(s) we are trying to achieve. Sometimes during the course of therapy the answers to these questions change. Flexibility, as always, is essential.

Betty found the answers to these questions as she began to experience healing and feel more powerful. The anger that had been so threatening to people who had worked with her in the past began to take the shape of a plan for positive action. Betty discovered as she went over the events of her life, most of which had been hurtful to her—a bad marriage, abuse of her daughter, alcoholism, suicide attempts—that she had an overwhelming desire for her father to experience the consequences of his abuse.

When Betty had left the family and gone on to even more victimization outside, her father had continued his life, his work, his relationships in a normal fashion. No one knew of the terrible things he had done to his daughter. His secret was safe, and so was he. Betty found this intolerable. She wanted something more to happen so she could finally free herself from the all-consuming and destructive anger that was so central to her life.

As part of her healing process, Betty had made a commitment to try to help other victims become survivors as she had so powerfully done. Betty's solution to both issues, the rage at her father and her need to help others, became a single course of action. Betty knew that I was involved in local television programming. She asked whether I would be interested in interviewing her and giving her an opportunity to tell her story publicly. There's a saying, "You're only as sick as your secrets," and Betty had decided that she was not going to keep this secret anymore. If her father or anyone he knew happened to see the tape, then Betty felt that some of the shame, humiliation, and pain she had endured would be visited upon him.

For Betty this was a powerful move. She had determined what it was that she needed in order to feel finished with this part of her recovery. She would be able to turn back upon her abuser the consequences of his actions and not have to continue suffering them herself. Betty and I worked on making this tape something positive, both for her and for other women who had been victimized, and not merely an act of vindictiveness. If that was the main objective of our efforts, then Betty would indeed still be a victim, one who had merely won the next round of an endless battle.

Betty did the tape. She was articulate, honest and open about her hurt and her healing. She took responsibility for the things in her life that were hers to own. She admitted that she had abused alcohol to dull the pain and find relief from the awfulness of her life, but she also pointed out that she had finally taken steps to turn this around. She talked about joining a twelve-step program, which had helped her remain sober for six years. She described the therapeutic journey from psychiatric hospitalization to individual therapy that empowered her to learn and grow. Betty's recovery has not ended by any means. She struggles each day to maintain her strength and her motivation to continue learning how to be a survivor. The wounds that Betty suffered were devastating and deep, but her scars are constant reminders that healing is possible. She shows them willingly to others who are bleeding so they will know what they can accomplish if they keep trying to get well. Betty is someone who took the power of her rage and turned it into something of value for herself and for other survivors. Her story is one of courage and hope: the courage to believe she could get well, and the hope that made her healing possible.

My Story

Some of the powerful moves that adult survivors make as they seek to heal may not be understood by those who have not had to struggle to survive the trauma of childhood sexual abuse. The way I claimed my power and became a stronger and more confident survivor is just one example. However, each person must find her own path to wellness and wholeness. I believe I did that and share part of my story in that spirit.

I was very close to my father from the time I was a young child. My father took me most places with him, he read to me every night and recited poetry, he sang songs and made jokes. My father taught me how to swim and how to cook. I always felt very loved and valued when I was with my father. I knew I was very special to him, and he was certainly very special to me.

This all changed when my father began to slip into my bed at night and molest my body. I was frightened and confused. I turned my head to the wall and wondered what was happening and what I could do to stop it. Finally, in desperation, not wanting to speak of this terrible thing, I took a bobby pin from my hair and chewed off the soft rubber tip. I then began to gouge the plaster wall next to my bed, and each night the damage to the wall became more obvious and ugly. No one ever mentioned the wall to me. No one ever scolded me or asked why I was ruining the wall next to my bed. My father continued to molest me, and the hole in the wall became bigger and bigger. He found other ways to violate my body, but I remained silent. My silence continued until many years later when as an adult survivor, I finally broke through this wall of denial I had begun chipping away for so many years. It was the beginning of a process that has led me to where I am today, no longer a victim who keeps silent but a survivor who finds power in the truth of my life and will not surrender that power or truth for anything or anyone.

From my earliest memories of my family, there were always two alliances: my father and me, and my mother and my brother. In healthy families there is supposed to be a union between the husband

and wife, father and mother, while the children form the sibling sub-system. In my family, a family that could be characterized as dysfunctional, this was not the case. I was my father's daughter and ally, while my mother doted on my brother and made him the center of her world.

This was a painful thing for me to live with as a child. I was confused about why my mother preferred my brother. Was it because I wasn't good enough, or pretty enough? Didn't I help her with the housework and try to make her proud of me by bringing home good report cards? Try as I would, I could never change this dynamic. I learned to accept it and live with it, and actually it wasn't so bad at first because I had the attention and support of my father, who was intelligent, witty, and fun to be with. It seemed to be a trade-off that was in my favor, so I tolerated the situation.

However, all that changed when my father began to molest me. Not only did I have to endure the confusion and humiliation of sexual abuse, but I had to endure it alone. My mother had never been my advocate, and I had no reason to believe anything would change if I told her of the abuse. Besides, my father was all I had in this family. Sides had been chosen long before, and he was the only player on my team. I couldn't risk losing my only parent, my sole ally. So the abuse continued, and I learned how to be a good victim.

I married at nineteen, more as a means to escape the family than anything else, and continued to keep my secret for many years. Finally, when I was thirty, I told someone of my abusive past and by breaking the silence, began my process of healing and empowerment. This process has taken many twists and turns. A lot of what I have learned has been through trial and error, following my instincts, and learning to identify situations and people that threaten to revictimize me. I have had to learn how to make choices and live with the consequences.

What I have found to be one of the most important ingredients in my efforts to be strong and confident is honesty. Child victims of sexual abuse are taught to repress the truth. They even learn to bend reality in order to live with the horror of their experiences. Perpetrators teach victims that the truth is something to be avoided and even feared. When I decided that I wanted to survive my abusive past and become a powerful, resourceful person, I knew that I had to embrace the truth in my life and live it as consistently as I could.

One of the truths of my family was that my mother had had room in her emotional life for only one of her children: her son. In fact, when my sister was born eleven years after me, my mother "gave" her to my aunt, the woman who had raised her after the death of her own mother. I learned to accept this fact, having no other choice, and after my father died at age forty-eight, and I was nine years married, it seemed less important to me that my mother was unavailable to anyone but my brother. My motto became "that's just the way it is," because I knew that I could not change what had always been and probably always would be. The sting of this loss never went away, but it became tolerable with time.

While I continued to work on becoming even more honest in my life and dealing as best I could with the consequences of that honesty, I never considered challenging my mother about her choice to give her all to my brother and literally abandon her daughters. "That's just the way it was." I had broken the silence about my sexual victimization by my father and had even spoken to an audience of half a million on a popular television program about it. By being honest about what I had gone through, I had been able to move forward and become a survivor rather than a victim. But I continued to play a game with my mother and join in her fantasy that she had been a wonderful, caring mother to all three of her children. I spared her the truth and in so doing, I continued to play the role of victim.

There are many ways one gets stuck being a victim. One of the most hurtful and destructive ways is repressing the truth for the sake of another. In a disabled family children learn to do all kinds of things to protect the less able, and believe they are holding the family together by putting their own needs aside. Usually this is the case. However, survivors must learn, sometimes for the first time, that if they are to take responsibility for their lives, they must allow others to assume responsibility, like it or not, for their lives.

When I came to this realization, I knew that I had to be honest with my mother about what my childhood had been like. Somehow she had missed it, and I had helped her by dancing around the truth for so many years. I didn't know what I was going to do or what I was going to say, but shortly thereafter a situation presented itself where I had the opportunity to be more honest with my mother than I had ever been.

It seems that she was having a difficult time financially, and her stepson had called to ask if my sister and I would be willing to send my mother and her husband a sum of money each month to help them out. My first response was to agree, but with my newfound commitment to honesty and truthfulness, I told my mother during a subsequent conversation that she should sell her home in New Hampshire, which would significantly change her financial situation. A few years prior, she had moved to Nevada and had allowed my brother to assume "ownership" of her house. No one had said anything about it at the time because "that's just the way it was," and when it came to my mother and brother, you just accepted whatever happened. However, this was a new day, and the truth had come to be a critical part of my survival.

Up to this time, I should add, my mother and I enjoyed a very cordial relationship. We spoke regularly on the phone, and she wrote long, newsy letters from the new home in Nevada. My husband and I even made the trip from Massachusetts to Nevada one year and spent a few days visiting my mother and stepfather and seeing the sights. The relationship was not genuinely warm and close, although from all outward appearances, it seemed to be good, if not ideal. I had learned well how to play the game of "let's pretend" and found that what my mother and I had was better than nothing at all. Again it is not unusual for people who come from dysfunctional families to settle for what they have, no matter how inadequate or even hurtful it may be.

At this point I was at an important crossroad in my life and my process of healing. I wanted and needed to be honest with my mother about the hardships and pain I had experienced as a child growing up in a difficult family. I knew that telling her the truth would overcome one of the last obstacles to accepting my life in its totality: the good, the bad, and the ugly. However, I also knew that the choices that I made affected other people, and it was my responsibility to consider this. Since victims of childhood sexual abuse have no choice about their victimization and have to learn as adults how to make critical choices, this issue is a crucial one. When, for instance I make a choice that may impact another, I have to consider whether I am taking that person's ability to choose away from him or her and thereby repeat the sexual abuse dynamic.

I thought long and hard about how to tell my mother what had for so long remained buried and ignored. Finally I reached a decision to give my mother the choice about whether she wanted to hear what I needed to tell her. Carefully and thoughtfully I wrote her a letter. It seems easier to include that letter rather than try to describe it. Before you read the letter, though, you should be aware that I have never for one moment regretted making this move, a move that I believe was one of the more honest and powerful ones I have ever made. It felt right then, and it feels right now.

I have learned that living with fantasy or secrets or pretense is not living authentically. It reinforces all the negative and destructive things that survivors seek to overcome. It fosters feelings of helplessness and impotence, and these feelings are too close to what a survivor felt as a victim to be tolerated. Sometimes in order to gain something you need, you have to be willing to give up something else. That's part of the price you pay for living as fully and powerfully as you can. Each survivor must make her own choice about how she will live, what she will keep and what she is willing to give up. I have made mine, and although my choices may not be right for other survivors, I rejoice in the fact that I am able to decide what I need in my life and not leave that choice to someone else.

February 5, 1989
23 Charles Street
Westboro, MA 01581

Dear Mom,

I've taken some time to decide what I should write to you about why I've been reluctant to be in touch. As you may recall, some months ago we spoke on the phone and the issue came up about your selling the house in Nashua. I felt, and still feel, that it doesn't make much sense for you and Jim to be living on a restricted budget when you have property that would allow you to have an easier time of it financially. Of course I understand your position. It is, after all, a position that has existed for as long as I can remember, and it concerns your relationship with Kenny. That conversation, combined with your immediate communication with both Lori and Kristen to defend and praise Ken, brought up a lot of old, and as yet unresolved, issues for me.

At first I was going to sit down and write an honest and detailed account of my feelings that obviously go back a long way. I wanted to let you know how and why I'm angry and why, finally, after all these years, I can allow myself to express that anger and frustration. For many years I accepted the situation by saying: "Well, that's the way it is," but now I'm not quite so willing to do that, and I don't believe I should. I've come too far at too great a cost to ever accept negative situations without responding to them in some way. I'm deliberately being general and not specific because my decision is to be "up front" about the fact that I'm angry, but also to give you the choice about whether or not you want to know WHY. I should tell you to ease your anxiety that my anger is not the result of any sexual abuse by my brother. While there was considerable physical abuse and emotional abuse by my brother, the sexual abuse I suffered in our home was perpetrated by my father as I explained to you five years ago before I told my story on television.

I'm giving you the choice at this point because, while I do not intend to repress again the reality of what I had to live with growing up in our family and continue to see played out even now, I will not impose my reality on you without your choosing to know what I have to say. Perhaps from your perspective it would be better if all of this just went away and no one brought up any unpleasantness; from my standpoint it is such a healthy and positive thing for me to face the reality I've known and use it, hopefully, to enhance my relationships. It's up to you. If you would be willing to hear what I have to say, then I would be more than willing to share it.

My understanding is that you have the impression that I am having some health problems, given what you wrote to one of the children. Nothing could be further from the truth. Some months ago I had a D & C because I was having some difficulty, and the procedure proved that there was nothing wrong and resolved the problem immediately. I've never felt better, and I've never felt stronger. Life is going very well for me, for which I am very grateful. It's probably for that very reason that I'm able to deal with all of this finally. It feels very good and very necessary. What is good and necessary for you remains to be seen and is, as it should be, your choice.

We hope that you are well and happy. Whether or not you are aware of it at this time, I wish you no unhappiness and do not want to cause you any anxiety or pain. If you are open to communicating about this and willing to learn how I've felt and continue to feel about a number of issues, my brother being primary, then I welcome the opportunity to pursue this further.

Always,

Gretchen

I never heard from my mother again.

Step 5 Know sexual abuse survivors who claimed their power.

Women who were sexually abused, recovered, and became powerful:

Oprah Winfrey

Roseanne Arnold

Marilyn Van Derbur Atler

Maya Angelou

Patty Duke

Others:

As you learn of other women, add them to the list as they join you in claiming your power.

A Powerful
Model

6

It pleases me to ponder this message. It pleases me to think I'm communing with her, this unknown woman. For she is unknown; or if known, she has never been mentioned to me. It pleases me to know that her taboo message made it through, to at least one other person, washed itself up on the wall of my cupboard was opened and read by me. Sometimes I repeat the works to myself. They give me a small joy.

—*Margaret Atwood,* The Handmaid's Tale

When you hear some of the stories women tell about their abuse, you wonder how they have managed to survive their experiences much less go on to lead fulfilling, productive, and meaningful lives. Of course many of them don't. The damage they suffered, the memories of the abuse, and the dysfunction that results from it very often destroy the victims of abuse and leave them incapable of living a healthy, happy life. It's not hard to understand why this is so; what is more difficult to comprehend is how someone can survive the horror of torturous abuse and become a powerful example of the indestructibility of the human spirit.

Such a person is the woman whose story you are about to hear. Sara MacPherson suffered humiliating and harrowing sexual abuse, was the victim of cruel and painful physical abuse, and was emotionally battered for all her formative years and beyond. Sara was without comfort and protection throughout the many years she was being victimized; she suffered alone and believed that she deserved all the abuse she received.

Sara's story is horrifying but true. You may want or need to believe that such things can't happen; they shouldn't, but unfortunately they can. There are many stories such as Sara's that could be told. You may have even heard some of these stories or even lived them. All too often women are so severely abused that they cannot find the strength or the will to recover, and their stories die with them. We grieve their loss.

That's all the more reason for Sara's story to be told and told as honestly and vividly as possible. It's important because Sara is an inspiration for other women who have been abused. She clearly illustrates that it is possible for any abuse victim to be a powerful, strong, recovered person.

I interviewed Sara and decided that I would let her tell her story in her own words, as truthfully as she knows how. She has worked long and hard to survive the pain of the abuse she suffered, and part of her recovery has involved telling her story so she can be a guide and help for others. Most importantly, Sara wants to break the terrible cycle of abuse not only in her life and the lives of her children, but for all of us. I introduce you to Sara MacPherson:

> My earliest memory of abuse goes back to lying in my crib. I remember staring at the ceiling and hearing the sound of a truck pulling up in front of the house. I knew the sound of that particular truck. It was something that just went right through my bones. Then I could hear, along the walkway beside the house, the clink of milk bottles going past my window. I knew, I knew what was going to happen next. I knew that within minutes my mother and the milkman would be in my bedroom, and they would sexually assault me.
>
> I was unaware at the time, of course, that it was a sexual assault. I knew only that it was pain, severe pain. They would come in my room, and my mother would have one of those huge, red enema or douche bags, and they would rape me with that. They would fill me with liquid, and as my mother was doing that, she would chant that I was making her do it; she was doing it because I was bad, I was a horrible child, and I never should have been born. It was all my fault; over and over she would repeat that it was my fault, that I was making her do this to me.
>
> I was powerless. I could only lie there and wait for it to stop. It was horrible, absolutely horrible. It left me legacies, things like a horrible fear of the sound of glass clinking. That's a sound that to this day runs right through me, and I can't tolerate it.
>
> When I was very young—I was the youngest of four children—I thought I was the only one who was being abused in that way. I thought that my sisters, because they went to school, were able to escape that abuse, so I always held onto the hope that my salvation would come when I went to school. I thought for sure that when I went to school, I would be valuable to this family, and they would love and appreciate me because I would learn things. I thought that learning to read would be the key to my escape because my sisters could read, and that seemed very important to my mother. She valued my sisters because they could read . . . they seemed smart. I thought if

I could just be smart enough, if I could learn to read fast enough, she'd love me, too.

So I went to school. I was sent to a parochial school, and I was so excited. I was excited because it got me away from my mother for the first time in my life, and that was wonderful. I thought that would be the end of bad things happening to me. Up until this time my mother had been abusing me physically and emotionally. She abused me in absolutely every way. She actively abused me sexually until I was about four years old; then it tapered down to things like insisting upon giving me a bath until I was in the sixth grade.

So when I went to school, I thought: "This will be the answer for me." I had such hope when I walked into school that first day. Of course the nuns passed out your catechism the first day of school, and I was so anxious to find my salvation in that catechism. It was my first book and I opened that book, just opened it to a random page, and there was an illustration of sin. The illustration that they had used was milk bottles. The milk bottles that were free of sin were nice, clean, white, shiny milk bottles. Those that had some sins had little black spots in the milk bottles. But those that had mortal sin and were doomed to hell forever were empty bottles, like the ones the milkman carried away after he had molested me.

I felt destroyed. I felt absolutely destroyed by that image, and I knew at that point in my young six-year-old mind that I was doomed. I was doomed, and there was no hope. Everybody must know about me, and it was okay with everybody. After all, my mother kept telling me I was the devil's child, and my only choice at that time was to accept that fact because that's what I had been told, and that's what I had been taught. And now my salvation, the place that was supposed to save me, had reinforced that. I was devastated. But aside from that experience, school offered me the opportunity to meet other people and form positive relationships. I came home from school that first day with a lot of different things to think about. I sat down at the table for lunch, and my mother asked, "What happened in school today?" I was so very excited because I had met this little boy whose name I will never forget—Bobby Randall—who sat next to me in the first grade. I told my mother how wonderful that boy was and that I was going to grow up and marry him. Across the table came a hand, which just smashed me in the face. My mother then told me, "Don't ever, ever tell anyone how you feel. If you tell people how you feel, they'll have power over you, and they'll be able to control you. Don't ever tell anyone how you feel."

That was the lesson of my lifetime. I was crushed by that, just crushed. My whole thought that this school was going to save me was dashed. Between the catechism with the pictures of the milk bottles and my mother's "Don't tell anyone how you feel," I was in despair . . . absolute despair.

Images of those milk bottles returned to me at different times. When I was about fifteen years old, my older sister got married. I was so excited. I was a young, adolescent girl, and I got to wear this long, beautiful blue gown. I was one of my sister's bridesmaids, and I felt really special. For the first time that I can ever remember, I felt special. I felt like I belonged to that day, and that felt unusual to me because I never believed I belonged to anything. So that day was really important to me. Then came the wedding reception. I was up at the head table having a wonderful time. I was fully aware of the implications of my sister getting married. The sexual overtones of that mystified and excited me at the same time. All of a sudden the guests at the wedding clinked their glasses with their spoons in the standard call for the bride and groom to kiss. I freaked out. I simply freaked out. I didn't know how to handle it. It was like instant recognition that everybody must know what had happened to me because they were making that sound, and it was okay with them. All those people were clinking their glasses, and that was certainly an indication that there was nothing for me to be ashamed of, that what had happened to me should have happened because I was the devil's child.

So again I was devastated. I swallowed all of this. I swallowed the anger, all the rage I should have felt, and I let it rule my life. I had no self-esteem—nothing. I fully believed that everything my mother had taught me was true. What other choice does a child have when this is your only family?

I was a very isolated child, and this was by my mother's choice and by her design. Whenever I would develop a relationship with someone, make a friend, my mother would sabotage it. She would say things like, "Don't go to Mary's house. There's something wrong with her family. I don't like the way her family behaves." So being isolated, I had no frame of reference to judge what was going on in my family. I didn't know what to expect in a relationship. Normal to me meant the abusive, aberrant behavior I knew from my experience. I didn't know what was good, what was positive. I had nothing to base an evaluation on.

For instance we had a ritual in my family on Sunday mornings. We'd all go to church together and then come home to a nice, sit-down breakfast. After breakfast I was made to go into my parents' room and lie down on my father's bed, and my father would come in and tickle me. He would tickle me until I cried and screamed. It was a Sunday morning ritual, but not the kind of thing between a father and daughter that was playful and fun. It was, "You must be in there. You must be in there on time, and you must be lying prone on that bed." The tickling was for my father's enjoyment. I would say, "Please don't do it. Stop, stop, stop!" My father would tell me, "You're my kid. I can do whatever I want." It was sadistic.

I've also begun to remember times when my father would molest me, and that is the hardest thing I've had to remember. It's like the last frontier of my remembering. My father used to tell me that he loved me, and I needed someone in my life who cared about me. To give up that illusion is the hardest thing I've ever done.

I have memories of my father standing over me in my sisters' bedroom and making me molest them. He made me perform sexual acts on my sisters while he stood by. I was about six or seven, and my sisters were twelve and fourteen. I felt such horrible, horrible shame along with it.

All this time my family appeared to the world like the typical American family. They were very involved with the community; they were very involved in the schools. They were extremely involved in the church. My mother was religious to the point of being fanatical. In fact on Sunday evenings at 7:00 P.M. the rosary would come on the radio and we had to kneel down and say the rosary. My mother would almost wail the prayers. It was scary, very scary.

The typical American family all right. I've spent years trying to recover from what I went through in this family. Aside from the sexual abuse, which was traumatizing in itself, I'm still suffering the effects of the physical abuse I experienced. One of my mother's ways of disciplining was to yank your arm until the bone would dislocate. My brother was three years older than I, and by the time I was three and he was six, we were able to relocate each other's bones because we were never taken to the hospital. We just had to live with it. I know that I had bones broken as a child because I've had X-rays taken since and found that there were bones broken and never set.

I went for some dental work recently, and the dentist said, "What the heck happened to you? Were you in an accident or something? You've got fractures all over your jaw?" I can only assume those were from the abuse because I was never in an accident. So I have fractures in my face that are irreparable, I've had seven surgeries so far to correct abdominal scar tissue, and I've had a hysterectomy because my uterus was so damaged. My pregnancies before the hysterectomy were very difficult also because of the condition of my uterus. My first child was born six weeks early after a very "at risk" pregnancy, and my recovery was hard.

There's more, much more, but this should give you some idea of what I experienced as a victim of child abuse. It's taken me many years to deal with the effects of this abuse, and I have suffered many losses along the way. Right now I have a wonderful, supportive husband and two precious children, but I have no other family. When I made the choice to speak out against the violence I knew as a child and also to advocate for my children, the price I paid was the loss of my family. It's painful to realize that, in a sense, I am an orphan in this world, but I wouldn't change a thing. I am a strong, resourceful person at this point in my life, and I'm nobody's victim anymore. I feel a personal power that has helped me do remarkable things and even encourage others to move beyond victimization to health and happiness.

My childhood was a tragedy. My life now is filled with goodness and love and contentment. By that I don't mean that life is always easy. Quite the contrary. My experience as a victim of abuse makes it harder sometimes for me to claim my power and to use it in my life. But I have the ability to deal with what comes along and to transcend all the pain in order to move forward to better things.

I am not bitter. I refuse to allow myself to be eaten up by resentment and rage. My anger is channeled into the work I do, and I use its power, hopefully, to change the world and break the cycle of abuse for others. I am a fortunate woman.

Now that you've heard Sara's story (and, believe it or not, that's only part of the abuse she suffered) and you've seen how strong and healthy she is, I think you can understand what a powerful example she is for those who have known the trauma of victimization. Sara learned how to tap into her power and use it to enhance her life and the lives of others. This transformation is possible for anyone. Sara is a special person, but she's not unique in her ability to heal and be transformed. In the next chapter you will learn how she was able to rise above the awful abuse she suffered as a child and of the fateful circumstance that compelled her to claim her power and become a model for other survivors who need to find out, as Sara often said, "Defeat is not an option."

Step 6 Give yourself powerful, positive messages.

Each day choose a phrase to repeat to yourself at least ten times. These are some suggestions, but you can add your own that have special meaning and effectiveness for you.

- I can do it.
- Defeat is not an option.
- My life belongs to me.
- I will not give up my power.
- No one controls my life but me.
- I make the choices. I take the consequences.
- I will not be a victim.
- I choose to live better.
- I set my own boundaries.

The Power
of Transformation

7

A man found a cocoon of the emperor moth and took it home to observe the process of transformation. One day he noticed a small opening through which the moth was trying to emerge. The hours went by and eventually, afraid that the moth would die, the man cut the cocoon open so that the moth could be free. To his surprise, the moth with its huge swollen body and shriveled wings was never able to fly and soon died. The struggle to emerge from the cocoon turned out to be a necessary step in forcing fluid from the body into the wings. In trying to ease its passage, the man had actually prevented the moth from gaining full control of its powers.

—Linda Weltner

Sara MacPherson suffered a life of unspeakable abuse as you learned in the last chapter. Her life was one of struggling to escape the pain she had been forced to endure, trying to understand, if she could, the reasons for her family's cruelty, and attempting to heal from it all.

Sara survived the abuse with a deep and abiding resolve not to let the trauma she had experienced defeat her and, most importantly, Sara was determined to protect her children from the kind of life she had known as a child. She vowed that her daughters would never be victims of abuse—she would see to that. Sara's life was dedicated to this promise, a promise she ironically found she could not keep.

Ali was the first child to come to Sara with the devastating information that she had been sexually assaulted by her uncle, the husband of Sara's sister, while she had been visiting the family. Shortly thereafter, Jean, the youngest of the two girls, admitted that the same thing had happened to her two years before, and that she had been too confused and ashamed to tell her parents.

Sara's worst nightmare had come true. Her children, so innocent, so beautiful, so vulnerable, had been violated by the uncle they had loved and trusted. Sara and her husband were outraged and knew that they couldn't ignore this situation. They knew enough about perpetrators of this kind of abuse to be aware that it doesn't usually stop until someone or something intervenes to put an end to it. They also believed that people who commit this kind of injustice, or indeed any kind of wrongdoing, should have the consequences of their acts visited upon them and not upon their victims. Sara knew this all too well, having suffered the effects of her own abuse while the victimizers had gone on with their lives without skipping a beat.

When Sara had been victimized, there was no one, or at least Sara had thought there was no one, she could turn to for protection or for justice. Jean and Ali, however, had a mother and father who were not about to let this situation go unreported or unresolved. This was an important and powerful message for Jean and Ali. It was also an important first step in their own process of transformation, and one which Sara had never had in her life.

So Sara and her husband reported the assaults to social services and brought the girls to a therapist to deal with their trauma and get the support they needed through the long and difficult process of bringing their abuser to justice. The next step was to work with the state as they brought charges against Sara's brother-in-law. That was not an easy decision since Sara's family, and particularly Sara's sister, angrily opposed this move. They isolated Sara and her family and thereby created yet more losses for them to deal with. A dysfunctional family may not be the best family one could wish for, but if it's your family, it's all you've got. When you give up your family, dysfunctional as they may be, you also give up the hope that someday, somehow things will all get better.

Sara and her children bravely persisted. They persisted through court appearances, and the giving of statements that caused them to relive their humiliation and fear. They persisted in spite of rejection by family and some friends. Every legal postponement was disappointing and delayed the process of closure and healing.

Finally the trial took place, and the girls were able to tell what had happened to them to a judge in a court of law. The guilty verdict did much to help the girls heal from their ordeal so that they could get beyond this tragic episode and deal with the aftermath.

This is where the story should have ended—with vindication and justice won. But it didn't. The perpetrator of this shameful crime of molesting his nieces appealed the verdict, as was his right, and the guilty verdict was overturned. Defense attorneys use whatever they can, hopefully of a legitimate nature, to prove the innocence of their clients. This defense attorney argued that because Jean, the oldest girl, was dyslexic she obviously had been confused and had mistaken a very innocent situation for a sexual assault. The jury must have agreed because they acquitted the abuser, exonerating the girls' uncle of any wrongdoing. This dyslexic, confused, and mistaken young woman, incidentally, was recently inducted into the National Honor Society. So much for her inability to understand and interpret reality.

Can you imagine the anger and disappointment of this family? Sara and her family felt powerless, bereft, abandoned by the very system that is supposed to intervene appropriately when laws are broken. They had to struggle for so long and so hard to do what was right, not just for themselves, but for all the potential victims that might be in jeopardy from this man. Instead of being punished for this awful deed, this criminal had just had his behavior sanctioned and reinforced.

Ali and Jean had believed that if their uncle, the man who had abused them, was made to suffer the consequences of his actions, they would not have to. Now they were left with feelings of confusion and a deep mistrust of the system they had trusted to help them. However, they also had the knowledge that they had done the right thing for themselves. They had spoken of their abuse, refused to take responsibility for what was the fault of their abuser, and tried to stop the cycle of abuse their uncle was actively engaged in.

Ali and Jean, although they had also been abused by a family member, found that their experience was vastly different from their mother's. Sara had suffered alone and isolated, never able to confront her victimizers, stop the abuse, and cause the consequences to be visited upon them. Ali and Jean had the loving support of their parents and the opportunity to bring their abuser to justice, although the outcome should have been different.

The cycle of abuse which had victimized Sara was indeed broken and an important transformation occurred as a result. First of all, Sara's pain and suffering were transformed into power, a power that enabled her to stand up against the wrong that had been done to her children. She was able to infuse her children with courage and confidence and help them achieve a justice of sorts. Once they were able to look beyond the inequity of what they had experienced in court, they could appreciate the fact that they had spoken out about their assault and against the perpetrator, tried under taxing circumstances to bring him to justice, and now could heal from everything that had happened.

It gets better. When the family was at their lowest point trying to find answers to questions they couldn't understand, when they were dealing with all the painful issues that victims have to contend with, they wondered what resources were available for other victims. The question that presented itself over and over was, "What help is there for other victims who may not have all the love and support we have in this family?" The answer was, "Not much."

It was then that Sara decided she could use her power as a survivor, along with the help of her family, to form an organization for victims and their families that would help them with whatever they needed. Gradually Victim Advocates United emerged with Sara in the forefront. She gathered others to her who believed as she did that abuse cannot go unanswered, and that victims need to help one another so that no one will have to go through what Sara and her family experienced.

It was yet another powerful transformation for Sara. The organization grew slowly but steadily. Victim Advocates United, a non-profit organization, began to provide services such as counseling, referral, support, and encouragement to anyone who needed their assistance. Sara engaged people to speak to groups like the police, the schools, the churches, and any other group that wanted to know about abuse and how to prevent it.

At this point in time, the organization continues to grow, funded by private donations and grants. Sara works tirelessly in whatever capacity is necessary to get her message across that abuse of anyone in society is wrong and must be stopped. She also inspires and encourages people who have been victimized to claim their power and become the strong and resourceful people they can be.

This transformation in Sara's life has touched a great many people, especially Sara's daughters, Ali and Jean, who continue to find ways to develop their own personal power. Already they have generated an energy that has helped them accomplish amazing things for two young women who are now part of the survivor population. In a real sense Jean and Ali exemplify two important and powerful messages. First of all, Jean and Ali have been able to achieve many of the things they've done because they have an excellent example in their mother, who survived her abuse and claimed her power. Secondly, they transformed their own situation into one of power in their lives and are helping others, both young and older survivors of abuse, to find their individual inner strengths.

Both girls have decided to share their stories and their transformation with others. It's their way of helping to break the cycle of abuse. A while ago, Sara had an opportunity to become involved in making a documentary about sexual abuse. She welcomed the occasion and offered her daughters the chance to talk about their experiences from victimization to healing. The girls were delighted and joined other survivors in making the documentary, which helped once more to bring the issue into the open. The video was nominated for five national and one international award, but aside from that, it gave people some important information and increased awareness about abuse.

The girls learned, through the example of their mother, that a large part of the healing process for a survivor of sexual abuse is in reaching out to other survivors and sharing the process of recovery. Jean found this to be true by participating in the video documentary. So when her teacher announced to her seventh grade class that there was to be an essay contest sponsored by an academic magazine, Jean knew right away what she would write about: she would write about her abuse and what she had learned. Her message would be a positive one which underlined the value of a healthy, loving, supportive family.

When her teacher learned what Jean had chosen to write about, she told Jean that it was not an appropriate subject for her and that she should choose another. Jean, believing that her message was important and perfectly appropriate, did not buckle under the weight of the teacher's authority. She wrote her essay, much to the chagrin of her teacher, and submitted it to the contest. All the while, Sara, incensed by the teacher's lack of sensitivity and understanding, remained in the background while her daughter forged ahead under the power of her inner convictions. Sara knew that her daughter had an excellent opportunity to learn the art of making her own choices through a thoughtful and reasoned examination of the facts. She also knew that it was important for Jean to learn how to deal effectively with powerful people and not to be intimidated into giving up or giving in.

Sometimes things work out. Jean opened the letter from the magazine that was sponsoring the contest and learned that her essay had made it to the final stage and that she would be notified of the committee's decision in a few weeks. When the notification finally arrived, Jean was informed that her essay had earned an honorable mention, a considerable feat for a youngster competing in a nationwide writing competition.

Jean couldn't wait to show her teacher the letter. She wasn't quite gloating, but it was hard to tell the difference between pride and gloating. Let's just say that she deserved to gloat a bit over this amazing accomplishment achieved against all odds.

The teacher congratulated her with little enthusiasm and asked if Jean and her family were planning to attend the award ceremony in New York. As if they would miss it. They went and proudly stood together as they shared this moment that had a very special meaning for this very special family. Sometimes in life we are given a moment when everything comes together in a way almost impossible to describe. For Jean and her family, this particular moment was a time when they knew they had transformed all the trauma, disappointment, and rage that they had experienced as a family, and they felt an elation that comes from victory.

Jean and Ali and their mother, Sara, will not be victims again because they don't know how to be powerful when faced with negative situations. They are also teaching others what they know to be true: personal power, when used appropriately and well, can transform your life and the lives of others. Jean and Ali give us all hope that the cycle of victimization can be broken before anyone has to suffer years of unhappiness and repeated abuse.

Sara MacPherson claimed her power, and when she did, she became an example to her daughters of what is possible. She taught them how to use their resources and to make crucial choices in their lives. She taught them the power of transformation.

QUESTIONNAIRE

Step 7 **Find your power.**

1. **Do you feel powerful?** _____

    When? _____

    How? _____

    With whom? _____

2. Do you feel powerless?_____

　　When?_____

　　How?_____

　　With Whom?_____

3. Do you remember a time in your life when you felt powerful?_____

　　When?_____

_____

4. In what areas of your life do you feel the most powerful?

_____

_____

5. In what areas of your life do you feel least powerful?

_____

_____

6. Do you know what resources you need in order to feel powerful?

　　What are they?_____

_____

7. Do you know how to get and to use these resources?_____

8. What changes can you make in your life in order to feel powerful?

_____

_____

9. Who and what can help you? _____

_____

If you find yourself changing from a powerless to a powerful person, try to remember when and how that change occurred. What did you do to make the transition? What resources did you tap into? Did you learn a process that you can use again when you are feeling powerless?

Note what you learned so you can use that information again when you need to be powerful and in charge of your life.

Claiming Your Power

8

. . . For women today, power may be defined as "the capacity to implement." A large part of this task is the implementation of the abilities women have already.

. . . Until now, women who are already strong in many ways still have had a hard time admitting it.

—*Jean Baker Miller,* Toward a New Psychology of Women

It seems obvious at this point that a personal sense of power is something we all need if we are to be successful and happy people. Merely talking and sharing our thoughts and feelings about power and powerlessness is not enough. We need some concrete guidelines to use as we struggle to be powerful and to have control of our lives. If we know the pitfalls of powerlessness, then we ought to know what to do to be powerful.

This chapter is an attempt to offer suggestions for claiming power and to look at ways to maintain that power consistently and positively. Each individual is unique and has a history and experiences that add different dimensions to this quest for personal power. What I will try to offer are general guidelines to consider and practice if they seem appropriate. Anything you build will have some structure and parameters; your life is no different. So consider the following:

•RECOGNIZE when you start to feel powerless. Often this will happen when you are faced with an important decision, need to confront a situation or an individual in your life, or are presented with an obstacle or a challenge. The signals may be feelings of depression, negativism, hopelessness or any number of other emotional responses that are unique to you and your experience of past victimization(s). Your body may feel weaker. You may want to run away or give up or allow someone else to take over. At times like these you need to call upon your resources, your personal power to effect a positive outcome, but first you have to be aware that you are sinking into a mire of powerlessness.

Remember that every time you become powerless, it's as if you have a neon sign above your head with an arrow that flashes "Victim, Victim, Victim." Remember, too, that somewhere (everywhere) is a would-be victimizer, who is constantly looking for that neon sign so he or she can gain a sense of power by manipulating someone less powerful.

•KNOW your own unique symptoms of powerlessness and the behaviors that follow ("Make it a double"). Some of us may indulge in escape fantasies when feeling powerless ("I'm leaving," or "It doesn't matter"). Knowledge is power. After a time your behavior or fantasies will have red flags attached to them, and as soon as you start to feel powerless, the red flags will alert you that you're falling into dangerous, destructive waters. Then you can do something about changing course and finding the power you need to meet your challenges.

•TAKE ACTION. One of the best ways to change a negative situation is to *do* something about it. The opposite of inaction is action. When you're beginning to feel powerless and to respond to these feelings by becoming powerless, do something. You may have to start with the smallest behavior or if you can't seem to make even one small positive step toward claiming your power, repeat to yourself: "I am not powerless over this. I am not powerless over this." Fuel yourself with positive energy and thoughts so that you can eventually do something about your situation. Be patient, be consistent. There will be days when you will run the race like an Olympic champion, and other days when you will crawl. The important thing is that you keep going in the right direction and don't drop out of the race.

•DON'T TAKE ACTION. Sometimes one of the most powerful things you can do is *not* take action, especially if to act would be negative or ill-advised. For instance, adults who were sexually abused as children often feel overly responsible for other people or situations. We are inveterate caretakers, always trying to make things better or keep people from hurting themselves and feeling pain (God forbid anyone should feel pain). To stand apart from someone and let things appropriately play out is a very difficult thing for sexual abuse victims. However, wisdom dictates in some situations that we do just that.

•KNOW THE DIFFERENCE. When is it important to take action, and when should you refrain from doing something in a given situation? It may take a few trial-and-error runs before you can see the difference between powerful action and powerful inaction. After the fact, you need to reflect honestly and sometimes painfully on what happened and try to *learn* how to respond or not respond better next time. You will make mistakes. If you keep working and try to learn from your mistakes, you *will* make fewer as you go along. Take the risk.

•CLAIM YOUR POWER. Your power is a special gift. It is your spirit, your energy source. There are people who cannot or will not find and use their power and will try to take yours. Sometimes you will all too willingly surrender your power to others in order to take care of them or help them become stronger. It may work, or appear to work, but it is never the best situation either for you or the "usurper of power." Power is like money in the bank. If it's not in your account, it's not yours. You may give your money away to another, but then it becomes your money that someone else has in his or her possession. You have no claim to it once you've given it away. Power works in much the same way. Some people fear having power because it can be used in destructive ways. But so can money.

Remember that the choice is yours. You can decide to use your resources to enhance your life and the lives of others, or you can misuse your power, your energy, or your financial resources. It's up to you. On the surface who would *choose* to be powerless? Who wants or needs to be powerless and vulnerable? Who wants others to make the decisions in their lives? Let's be honest about this; there are people who cannot give up the role of victim. They cannot find the strength, the power, to reverse some very profound learning experiences in their lives. They feel "comfortable" when they are powerless. The choice to be powerful requires one to work hard to maintain her freedom, her independent thinking, her hard-won level of self-esteem. It's not always easy. Some of us are not up to the challenge and, sadly, some of us cannot find the path that leads to successful living. Many of us feel that we don't deserve to be better. Some of us have even learned how to attach ourselves to people who are more powerful so we can go along for the ride. It seems easier, and sometimes it is, but usually there are high costs for this ride and not much control about where it will ultimately take us. Be in charge as much as possible, and don't give away your power. Keep it in the "power bank" and draw on it when you need to.

•BE PERSISTENT. On one occasion when Winston Churchill was asked to address the graduating class of a renowned boys' school in England, the speakers who preceded him waxed eloquent and long. Who could resist the opportunity to send a group of young, eager and impressionable children out into the world without the wisdom garnered by "the wise" over a lifetime of living and learning? It is said that Mr. Churchill, when finally given the opportunity to add his sage advice to that of the other speakers, approached the podium and proclaimed in a clear and resounding voice: "Never give in, never give in, never, never, never, never—in nothing great or small, large or petty—never give in except to convictions of honor and good sense." That is good advice for all of us, but particularly for those who struggle to overcome the powerlessness of victimization. You will not always be successful in claiming your power; there will be many obstacles put in your path, but never give in. Never give in. Never give in.

•WHAT ARE THE REWARDS? In his poem "Invictus," William Ernest Henley writes:

I am the master of my fate:
I am the captain of my soul.

Anyone who knows the joy of being in charge, in control of her life, knows how important these words are and how crucial it is to do everything possible to be the master of her destiny. Of course there are times when absolute and complete control is not possible. We all have to make necessary compromises; we don't live in isolation, but no one should determine how we will live from day to day or make the critical choices about our lives. How can you measure the feeling you have when you are free? What is it worth to be in charge of your life instead of under the control of another? Throughout history there is overwhelming evidence that people long to be free and will sacrifice just about anything, including their lives, for that freedom. Sexual-abuse victims know what it's like to be prisoners. Someone more "powerful" once put us in bondage, took away our choices, and kept us isolated from any would-be rescuers, if rescuers indeed existed. Some of us have lived in that prison for years and are just beginning to find a way out. But when those bonds are loosed, and we know the sweet feeling of no longer being the captive of our past or doomed to repeat it, there is a glorious, precious freedom that is ours. Is this worth fighting for? Is this worth continuing to remain vigilant lest we become victims again? Does claiming our power offer rewards that are worth the effort? What do you think?

Step 8 Claim your power.

1. Do you recognize when you are in a powerless position?
   Yes _____ No _____

2. What situations or people cause you to feel powerless?

   _____

3. How do you feel when you are powerless? (i.e., depressed, angry) _____

   _____

4. Are you able to gain power and control in your life by taking action?
   Yes _____ No _____

5. What "action behaviors" work best for you? _____

   _____

6. Are you unable to take action?
   Yes _____ No _____

7. What keeps you from taking action?_____

   _____

8. Can you remember a time when you felt powerful? What were your rewards?_____

If you have been unable to act in a powerful way or assume appropriate control of a situation, try the following exercise: Close your eyes and picture yourself in a difficult situation that you were unable to resolve successfully because you couldn't feel or be powerful. Try to imagine a more powerful approach that you might have taken. Visualize yourself making strong, bold moves, or if the situation suggests, make no move at all. Be successful, be powerful. Savor the feeling and consider making those similar moves when the next difficult situation arises in your life. Remember the feeling of power you had in your visualization, and claim your power so those actions and feelings will more and more become a reality in your life.

Power Is
a Choice

9

In the beginning was the word,
and the word was choice.

—*Tom Robbins*

Children who are sexually abused do not have a choice about their abuse. Their choice is taken away by the abuser, along with their developing sense of personal power. Choice and power are very connected for sexual-abuse victims, and when we speak of power, it is important to look at choice at the same time. If as a child you had been allowed to develop normally and gradually become more powerful and in control of your life, choice would not have been a factor in your understanding or use of power. Your sense of personal power would have evolved under the loving and supportive guidance of your caretakers. It would not have been necessary for you to choose whether you wanted or needed to be powerful. Your power would have grown and developed naturally and consistently throughout your formative years.

However, at this point, having survived the trauma of sexual abuse, having learned how not to be powerful, it's important, even necessary, for you to make a choice to be powerful and to use that power in positive ways. Perhaps now we can begin to understand power in ways that are relevant to us and to our individual lives as survivors. Power has been given a "bad rap," and it's easy to see why that is so. Many women, and all sexual-abuse survivors, have been victims of the misuse of power. To victims power is something to be feared, to be avoided. Power conjures up bad feelings, perhaps a sense of guilt. It is not seen as positive but as something harmful to be rejected. Power is also generally associated with the male gender, and many of us don't want to identify with the gender of the perpetrators of our abuse or risk harm in trying to take power from them. The bottom line is that victims are "taught" that power is not something available to them. Their victimization has shown them that there are two kinds of people:

those who have power and those who don't, and the latter are frequently the victims of power gone wrong.

The important thing for survivors to be aware of is that power is a choice: we can choose to be powerful. Sometimes it's an unconscious choice to either take or not take power and sometimes it's a conscious one. My personal opinion is that conscious choices can be changed. Having an awareness of why we behave in a certain way gives us an opportunity to behave differently—if we choose to. However, all is not lost if this information is unconscious. Then we have to work to bring our power issues to the conscious level, as the group did at the Rape Crisis Center in Israel, and make the decision to change.

As children who were victimized and learned that others made the choices that determined how we would live, we had no choice. Now we do, but we have to determine that we will take control of our lives and find the power that will allow us to accomplish all that we want and need to do. That in itself is a very powerful move. That decision "primes the pump." It's a way of establishing a direction, a vision that is ours. Power is not something that is going to fall out of the sky and land in our laps. We have to pursue it, and that's a difficult task, because going back and filling in the gaps in our lives is hard work.

The important thing to understand is that having a sense of personal empowerment and being able to act on that empowerment will insure that we will not become victims again. We will no longer be immobilized. We will make the choices in our lives and most of us would not choose to play the role of helpless victim.

This sense of power is what allows us to sleep soundly at night, feeling secure. This sense of power is what makes it possible for us to stand toe to toe with others who try to use their power to get their needs met at our expense, knowing that we have the ability to stand our ground. This power is the vindication of the abuse we suffered as victims. It says to us, "No more. You have choices in your life, and you can make them." This power is the chance to do things differently, to uplift and not degrade, to support and not sabotage, to use power in ways that enhance our lives and don't create more victims in this world.

If we learn how to develop and use the tremendous power that has been too long unavailable and denied to us, then we can go forward with our lives to get and to give, to achieve all our goals. We need to take all the negative energy that has ever backed up on us and caused us to be reckless and self-destructive and shape it into an energy that is positive and productive.

The fact is that our abuse and the other obstacles that we have had to overcome as a result of our trauma have enabled many of us to develop strengths and resources that we have not always recognized. We have acted up and acted out and managed to survive, but somehow we now need to redirect that energy and turn it into the power that we were denied as children.

Identify what it is you need or want in your life. Look within yourself to discover what resources you possess that can help you accomplish your goal. Look outside yourself and see what resources exist that you can tap into. Learn what obstacles you need to surmount in order to be successful. Be honest about your deficiencies so you can fill in those gaps as best you can. Then legitimately and appropriately claim your power as something that is yours, and go forward. You are not alone.

QUESTIONNAIRE

Step 9   Choose your power

1. Do you make most of the important choices in your life?

_____

2. If not, who does? _____

_____

3. Does this work well for you? _____

_____

4. What are three choices that were made recently?

a. _____

I made the choice ____ Someone else made the choice ____

b. _____

I made the choice ____ Someone else made the choice ____

c. _____

I made the choice ____ Someone else made the choice ____

5. Were you satisfied with the results of the choice?

_____

_____

6. If not, what obstacles stood in the way of a better choice
   being made?

_____

_____

_____

Imaging Exercise

Assume a relaxed position. Take ten long, deep breaths. Think of a positive, powerful phrase and repeat that phrase slowly to yourself three times. Picture in your mind what the obstacle or obstacles look like, such as a stone wall, a fence, barbed wire, whatever works best for you.

Begin to disassemble this obstacle while repeating your positive, powerful phrase. Piece by piece, section by section, remove parts of the obstacle. See the other side as a safe place, a non-threatening place. Picture it as somewhere you want to be. Picture a woman on the other side who is a powerful example for you, beckoning to you, encouraging you while you are doing the work you need to do to get there.

When the obstacle has been removed, take another ten long, deep breaths and open your eyes.

Using Your Power

10

The Guest is inside you, and also inside me;
you know the sprout is hidden inside the seed.
We are all struggling; none of us has gone far.
Let your arrogance go, and look around inside.

The blue sky opens out farther and farther,
the daily sense of failure goes away,
the damage I have done to myself fades,
a million suns come forward with light,
when I sit firmly in that world.

—Robert Bly, The Kabir Book

There are many positive ways in which you can use the power you've worked so long and hard to claim. These are just a few. The list is endless, and you will add to it each time you make the decision to be powerful. If a sense of empowerment is something new for you, you will have to work at it until it becomes internalized and as much a part of you as breathing. You won't always get it right. Sometimes you will fall back into old ways and feel comfortable in the land of powerlessness where you lived for so long, but begin again and try to learn with each experience what you might do differently. When J. C. Penney was asked what he thought the formula was for leading a successful life, he replied: "When you fall down, get up." It may be a simple rule, but if you follow it each day, you will get where you need to go.

The Power of Rage

There is a sense of being in anger. A reality
and presence. An awareness of worth. It is a
lovely surging.

—Toni Morrison, The Bluest Eye

Many people who come from dysfunctional homes where anger was out of control and destructive, reject anger and avoid it at all costs. The irony is that when you are appropriately angry at harmful people and negative situations, you are likely to avoid becoming a victim. Anger is a very powerful and useful emotion and legitimately should be part of the entire range of emotions that you express. Anger should not be suppressed and denied because it might be harmful. It should be used as a means to change situations that need changing or at least to express your dissatisfaction as powerfully as you can. If positive change comes about as a result of your voicing your anger, then you have accomplished something. However, if you do nothing more than feel relieved because you have expressed your honest feelings, that too is an accomplishment.

Look around you at the people who have been hurt or victimized; empathize with those who have been hurt or victimized and are angry about it. Many are consumed and destroyed by their anger, while others use anger to make positive changes in their lives or the lives of others. This use of rage is very productive and has traditionally created some very important changes in society. Rage is an energy that, when directed and focused appropriately, can be a force for good. Watch how others manage to use it this way—and learn from them.

While your victimization and the victimization of others is never justified, you have learned something about pain and anger and how it eats away at you when you are not able to advocate for yourself. Unexpressed rage often turns into depression which is a common malady for many people, particularly women. Women have suffered for years from the notion that to express anger is to be unladylike. Along with that stereotypical view is the belief that women who are able to silently endure pain and suffering are somehow more noble and brave. Most of us have grown up with those myths, and when we add to them the experience of being sexually abused as a young, powerless child, it's not hard to see why advocating for yourself is difficult.

If allowing yourself to be angry and to express that anger is a totally foreign experience for you, begin by noting those small violations or hurts that occur each day. If you aren't able to address them overtly or directly, think about how you would deal with them if you could. Let your imagination experiment with various approaches. Note which ones feel the most natural or right for you. Add to these scenarios a positive or beneficial outcome. Give yourself rewards such as praise and affirmation for handling things so well. Gradually you will feel powerful enough to try out in real life what you have practiced so well in your fantasy life. You don't have to start with enormous issues. Think of the process as a progression from a mental exercise to a small move and then to bigger and bigger challenges. Eventually you will be able to react to situations as they happen and to respond with whatever emotion you need to express. Anger is not always destructive—unless you keep it locked inside you and allow it to feed off your energy and your spirit. Use the power of your anger in ways that will enhance and not diminish your life. As Toni Morrison so beautifully described it, let your anger become for you "a reality and presence . . . an awareness of worth . . . a lovely surging."

The Power of Letting Go

> . . . *I've seen people who were very burdened with sorrows,*
> *in a sense, almost die from their sorrows. But I've also*
> *seen people who haven't had any sorrows at all die from*
> *the lack of them. I think it takes sorrow to open us to life.*
>
> —*Jess Lair,* I ain't much baby—but I'm all I've got

If you were a victim of abuse, you can never change that fact. Your experience had a tremendous effect upon your life. Even if the response of your caretakers was positive and supportive, sexual abuse is an event that always carries with it an element of harm. Sexual-abuse survivors learn how to be victims. Some people define their lives by their abuse, which is perfectly understandable. For instance, if you continue to play the role of victim with people, you learn a way of functioning in the world which becomes a way of life.

However, many survivors are beginning to learn new ways of acting that do not include being victimized consistently. It takes a great deal of effort and perhaps some time spent in therapy, but you can break the cycle of victimization. All you have to do is let go of your identity as a victim. Now that should be easy, right? Who wants to be a victim? Well, it's not so easy. Have you ever tried to learn a second language and found that it didn't happen overnight? Some people can't even master a second language and speak the language they learned as a child at the same time.

It's important to understand and be honest about the fact that there are some payoffs for being a victim. It's difficult to take responsibility for your life. It's hard to make choices and then live with the consequences of those choices. Sometimes it seems easier to let others take charge, make the decisions, be responsible. There are, according to some experts in the field of human behavior, some people who "prefer" being sick to being well because they can then avoid responsibility, gain sympathy, and allow others to do the world's work.

If you are to be a powerful person, to determine what you do with your life and with whom, then you must let go of the role of victim. You must forge a new identity, an identity that reflects your image as a survivor. There is power in that letting go, and unless you are able to let go in order to claim that power, you will continue to be a victim. Once you let go of your victim persona and the payoffs that come with it, you will experience a different kind of reward, one that will reinforce your "new language."

There is another kind of letting go that survivors oftentimes must face, and that is letting go of their families of origin. It is not unusual for families of sexual abuse victims, particularly when they are severely dysfunctional, to become enmeshed and remain connected with each other in ways that are not healthy or life enhancing. When a sexual-abuse survivor makes the choice to become strong and powerful, sometimes the last obstacle to her continued growth and well-being is her family. Even though the survivor may have changed for the better and learned new ways of living, that doesn't mean the entire family has changed. The family may still be trying to keep the survivor in the role of victim, requiring that she continue to live this way and punishing her when she refuses. Punishment can take the form of guilt, rejection, withdrawing of affection and support, anything that will bring the victim back into line with the family.

Many times I have worked with survivors who, while they have professionally and even personally done remarkable things in their lives, continue to be victimized by their families. They persist in suffering the pain of emotional abuse and even physical abuse as adults, and they feel powerless, just as they did as children, to walk away from that abuse or refuse to accept it. The reasons for this are not very complicated. Sexual abuse survivors frequently nurture the hope that their families will change. Someday their families will realize how special they are and embrace them with love and affection. All the hurt will melt away, all the sad and painful memories will be transformed into pearls of family togetherness and warmth. Somewhere in the heart of survivors is a Norman Rockwell painting of their family, waiting to leap from the canvas and become a reality.

Letting go of this fantasy is one of the most difficult things a survivor must accomplish, but it must be done if that is the only way she can stop being her family's victim or scapegoat. Sometimes a survivor will manage to become healthy and strong in every area of her life except her relationship with her family, but she will justify her hanging on because it's her family, after all, and you don't abandon your family.

In many instances the survivor is the glue that held the family together when she was the sacrificial victim. She learned this lesson well; she may have even felt important and necessary fulfilling this task. Rejecting the role of family victim initiates an enormous change, a change that the family will not tolerate. When one person changes her behavior in a dramatic way within the family, then all family members must by necessity change. People don't like to change, particularly people who lack strength and inner resources. The survivor then has a difficult choice to make. Does she maintain the fantasy that her family will one day become the healthy and loving family most of us read about and fewer people experience, or does she let go?

She lets go, and in letting go she reinforces in a very powerful way her deep and abiding commitment not to be a victim for anybody—not even her family. She proves to herself that her sanity, her peace of mind, her strength of purpose are her greatest gifts to herself, gifts that no one can take away.

Power of Forgiveness

So we shall ask: why forgive?
And we shall answer: because forgiving is the only way we
have to a better fairness in our unfair world; it is love's
unexpected revolution against unfair pain and it alone offers
strong hope for healing the hurts we so unfairly feel.

—*Lewis B. Smedes,* Forgive and Forget

When a sexual abuse survivor makes the choice to deal with her childhood victimization, she has the opportunity to confront the pain of her past and, hopefully, reframe her life in powerful, positive ways. Many challenges are presented to the adult survivor during this process, one of the most critical and complex being that of forgiveness.

It's difficult to think about forgiving someone who has done so much harm, created such havoc in the life of a powerless, trusting, and vulnerable child; a child who continues to suffer the consequences of her victimization as an adult. Perpetrators of sexual abuse are reviled and scorned by everyone who values decency and believes that children should be protected and nurtured and not hurt by their caretakers. It's common knowledge that the prisoners who are viewed with the most contempt by other prisoners and who are at very high risk of being harmed while in prison are the child molesters.

To further complicate the issue of forgiveness, many perpetrators, if not most of them, refuse to admit the wrongness of their act. They fail to take responsibility for the harm they have caused their victims, and the victims are deprived of the experience of having their offenders admit their guilt and ask for forgiveness.

However, forgiveness is probably the most important and powerful experience that an adult survivor needs to experience in some unique and personal way whether the abuser is involved or not. Forgiveness is not something that is done for the benefit of the abuser, although in some instances it may be mutually beneficial and healing. Forgiveness is for the survivor and is an act that allows her to unburden herself from the pain and suffering she has carried with her from childhood into adulthood. It is a release of negative energy that frees the survivor from the past and from the power that the abuser continues to hold over her life and her healing. Forgiveness means that victimization is no longer the dominant theme for the survivor and that the perpetrator of wrongdoing no longer has any power in her life. Forgiveness is a choice for the person who has been violated, a choice that is made in the process of healing when it is appropriate and right. As with any other choice that a survivor makes in her recovery, the timing of forgiveness is very important.

I remember clearly counseling a young woman who had been the victim of the most humiliating and degrading sexual abuse by her father. There is no act of sexual abuse that is acceptable or tolerable, but Diane's story was particularly gruesome. We had worked together many months on the issue of Diane's relationship with her husband, Steve. As much as Diane wanted to be part of a healthy, satisfying marriage, she was unable to accept the fact that the intimacy they shared was right and good. Her memories of the sexual abuse continued to intrude and obstruct her from fully participating in any aspect of the marriage that would require closeness or vulnerability. We were a long way from Diane reaching a point where she could forgive her father for the terrible acts he perpetrated on his daughter, but Diane had finally been able to tap into the anger she felt at having been a victim. The down side was that her husband, Steve, became the focus of that anger and their marriage suffered because of it.

During one session, I talked to Diane about this misplaced anger and of how it blocked her chances for getting close to Steve and having the kind of relationship she wanted as a survivor who had healed from the wounds of her past. Diane was either struck with an insight at that moment or had been aware all along of how the anger worked to her benefit. She said, "You don't understand. I need that anger to *keep* me from getting close to Steve or any man. I'm still afraid of being abused even though I know that it was my father who abused me and not Steve." Obviously Diane knew that she was not ready to let down the walls of anger that "protected" her from being hurt ever again. We had a lot more work to do.

If the anger that a survivor feels will not allow her to move on to the final stage of forgiveness, there may likely be a good and sufficient reason. Sometimes well-meaning people, friends, family, and counselors, encourage or even exert pressure on the survivor to rid herself of her anger and her painful memories by forgiving her abuser. Lewis Smedes who writes extensively about forgiveness says: "I think that anger and forgiving can live together in the same heart. You are not a failure at forgiving just because you are still angry that a painful wrong was done to you."

Forgiveness is not a quick fix or something that will make all the hurt and pain and the remembering go away. It is a profound act that is reserved for those who have been grievously hurt and need the balm of forgiveness to wash over their lives. Forgiveness releases the demons of hate, rage, vengeance, and malice and makes it possible for the survivor to fill herself with life-enhancing power and energy to go where she needs to go and get all she needs to get.

But what if the offender is dead, unavailable, or even unwilling to participate in the process of forgiveness? Can forgiveness be a solitary experience for the survivor of abuse? Absolutely! All forgiveness requires is that the person who was offended put aside her rage or other vengeful feelings and forgive the offender. Sometimes it takes an understanding and an awareness of the pain that the offender experienced that allowed the cycle of pain to continue. Sometimes it takes an honest examination of what the survivor clings to that makes forgiveness impossible and why it is necessary to hold on to whatever that is. Sometimes forgiveness occurs in subtle ways that go almost unnoticed. I know there came a time when I began to think of my father who had sexually abused me as a child in different ways. I no longer always thought of him as my abuser but began to remember how talented he was and of how he could build a house as easily as he could make an exquisite meal. I thought about what a wonderful sense of humor he had and of how people gravitated to him when he was in a crowd. I remembered, too, how troubled he was and of how he drank alcoholically for most of his life. I found myself feeling sorry for him and for his conflicted life which ended when he was a young man of forty-eight. These thoughts, loving and compassionate, cannot come into an unforgiving heart, so I know that I am no longer blaming or accusing but forgiving. I also feel that a burden has been lifted from my spirit that allows me to go forward with my life with less needless baggage to carry.

Whenever, as Smedes writes, you are looking at the person who hurt or offended you with new eyes, forgiveness is taking place. You may make the decision to forgive consciously or it may be an unconscious act born of a wisdom that resides in all of us that, when heeded, will cause us to do the right thing. Being able to forgive someone who has deeply hurt you and caused you great harm is one of the great mysteries of life. When a survivor of childhood sexual abuse forgives her offender, she takes part in that mystery and somehow comes to understand what a profound and powerful thing she has experienced and of how powerful she has become in the process.

The Power of Connectedness

My space chums are concerned about our evolvement because they say we're all connected. "Everything is part of everything." They started talking about a little something they call "interstellar interspecies symbiosis." To hold up my end of the conversation, I asked them to elaborate.

—Jane Wagner, The Search for Signs of Intelligent Life in the Universe

We are learning more each day about how many women were victims of sexual abuse as children. Women are talking about their experiences and learning with and from each other how to heal from their abuse and become powerful in their lives. While we lament the fact that so many women suffered sexual victimization during their formative years, we have come to understand that many of us are connected by this experience. There is a depth of understanding among survivors that can be used to initiate a number of positive changes for each other and for those still vulnerable to abuse. We can help break the cycle of abuse and insure that no child will suffer the trauma that millions of women have known over the years and still struggle to overcome.

There is some comfort and perhaps a sense of justice realized when survivors are able to transform or reframe their terrible experiences of childhood victimization into something positive. For many survivors this is the only way they can move forward, look beyond their trauma and deal with the pain they have experienced.

There is also a strength in connectedness that comes from knowing on many levels what another person has gone through and how that person has responded to life and relationships. This connectedness cannot be underestimated. Women who take part in support groups dealing with sexual victimization have learned that their own recovery is enhanced by working through issues with other survivors, by helping and being helped by them.

Many, many people have gained their strength, their sense of purpose, and their motivation by joining movements and causes around a common theme or mutual concern such as Mothers Against Drunk Driving, Alcoholics Anonymous, Recovery, to name just a few. One of the effects of this connectedness among survivors is the power that is beginning to be felt and acted upon by victims. Women are starting to stand up and speak out against the violence they've endured. They are attending rallies and talking about their experiences publicly and often painfully. Their hope is that their suffering will make society aware of the magnitude of the problem of abuse, help other survivors heal from their pain, and, hopefully, prevent others from being victimized at sometime in their lives.

The Power of the Truth

Many years ago as a young girl, I remember hearing a phrase that has never left me and has been the cornerstone of my life ever since. It was this wonderful and wise message, "The truth shall set you free." I wanted desperately to be free; free of all the pain and abuse in my family and free of my role as victim. I looked to anything and everything that would help me to know and to live the truth of my life so I could be free. I found that it was very simple. All you have to do is to be honest. It isn't always easy because oftentimes the truth is disguised or even hidden. It takes a lot of effort to seek it out and to doggedly pursue it even as it continues to elude you. But the search and its capture are worth it. There is a power in the owning and valuing of the truth. It is only when you know the truth of your life that you can be part of the world with all that you are, nothing lacking or hidden. Every part of you can participate in the experience of life and every part of you can feel this experience. You are whole when you own all of who and what you are and believe in all that you can be.

Don't be afraid of the truth. The truth is your best ally as you go through life. It is important to know who you are and what you are, where you came from and where you hope to go. The truth is what will help you to find your own personal power and strength and to make your life rich and full. The truth *will* set you free.

I hope you have found in this book some truth about your life that will help you take the critical step of claiming your power. As a survivor of childhood sexual abuse, you are not alone. You are connected to all the other survivors who know your pain and your sadness, and you are one with all of those survivors who know the joy and the victory of reclaiming their lives. We travel this road together.

> We came on this trek
> To find our life,
> For we are all,
> We are all,
> We are all the children of . . .
> A brilliantly colored flower,
> A flaming flower,
> And there is no one,
> There is no one,
> Who regrets what we are.
>
> —Huichol Indian Chant

QUESTIONNAIRE

Step 10   Use your power.

1. Can you use the power of rage? _____
   If not, why not? _____

   _____

   _____

2. Can you let go of your role as victim? _____
   If not, why not? _____

   _____

   _____

3. Have you forgiven your abuser? _____
   Why? _____

   _____

   Why not? _____

   _____

4. Can you feel like a whole person without forgiving your
   abuser(s)? _____
   Why not? _____

   _____

5. Do you feel connected with other survivors? _____
   In what way? _____

   _____

   If not, why not? _____

   _____

6. Can you accept the truth of your life? _____
   If not, why not? _____

   _____

7. In what way(s) do you use your power? _____

   _____

Reading List

Abraham, K. "The Experiencing of Sexual Traumas as a Form of Sexual Activity." *Selected Papers on Psychoanalysis.* London: Hogarth Press, 1907.

Allen, C. V. *Daddy's Girl.* New York: Berkeley Books, 1982.

Bass, E., and Davis, L. *The Courage to Heal: A Guide for Women Survivors of Child Sexual Abuse.* New York: Harper and Row, 1988.

Bass, E., and Thorton, L. *I Never Told Anyone: Writings by Women Survivors of Child Sexual Abuse.* New York: Harper and Row, 1983.

Becker, J. V.; Skinner, L. J.; Abel, G. S., et al. "Sexual Problems of Sexual Assault Survivors." *Women and Health* 9(4) (Winter 1984): 5–20.

Bender, L., and Blau, A. "The Reaction of Children to Sexual Relations with Adults." *American Journal of Orthopsychiatry* 7(1937): 500–18.

Bendict, H. *Recovery:How to Survive Sexual Assault for Women, Men, Teenagers, Their Friends and Families.* New York: Doubleday, 1985.

Boatman, B.; Borkan, E. L.; and Schetky, D. H. "Treatment of Child Victims of Incest." *The American Journal of Family Therapy* 9(4) (Winter 1981): 43–51.

Brady, K. *Father's Day.* New York: Dell Publishers, 1979.

Breur, Josef and Freud, Sigmund. *Studies on Hysteria, Complete Works.* Vol. II, 1896.

Idem. *Totem and Taboo.* Standard Edition, 13. London: Hogarth Press, 1955.

Brickman, J. "Feminist, Nonsexist, Traditional Models of Therapy: Implications for Working with Incest." *Women and Therapy* 3(1) (Spring 1984): 49–67.

Browning , D. H., and Boatman, B. "Incest: Children at Risk." *American Journal of Psychiatry* 134(1) (1977): 69–72.

Butler, S. *Conspiracy of Silence: The Trauma of Incest.* San Francisco: New Blide Press, 1978.

Chapman and Gates, eds. *The Victimization of Women.* Beverly Hills: Sage Publications, 1978.

Clarke, R. *Pastoral Care of Battered Women.* Philadelphia: Westminster, 1986.

Cole, E. "Sibling Incest: The Myth of Benign Sibling Incest." *Women and Therapy* 1(3) (Fall 1982): 79–89.

Cormier, B.; Kennedy, M.; and Sangowicz, J. "Psychodynamics of Father-Daughter Incest." *Canadian Psychiatric Journal* 7(1962): 203–17.

Courtois, C. A. *Healing the Incest Wound: Adult Survivors in Therapy.* New York: W. W. Norton and Company, 1988.

Daldin, H. "The Fate of the Sexually Abused Child." *Clinical Social Work Journal* 16 (Spring 1988): 22–31.

Dubreuil, G. "Les Bases Psycho-Culturelles du de l'Inceste." *Canadian Psychiatric Association Journal* 7(1962): 218.

Emslie, G. J., and Rosenfeld, A. "Incest Reported by Children andAdolescents Hospitalized for Severe Psychiatric Problems." *American Journal of Psychiatry,* 140:6 (June 1983): 708–11.

Faria, G., and Belohlavek, N. "Treating Female Adult Survivors of Childhood Incest." *Social Casework: The Journal of Contemporary Social Work* (1984): 465–71.

Feinauer, L. L. "Relationships of Long-term Effects of Childhood Sexual Abuse to Identity of the Offender: Family, Friend, or Stranger." *Women and Therapy* 7(4) (1988): 89–107.

Ferenczi, S. "Confusion of Tongues Between Adults and the Child." *International Journal of Psychoanalysis* 30(1949): 225–30.

Finkelhor, D. *Sexually Victimized Children.* New York: Free Press, 1979.

Idem. "Sex Among Siblings: A Survey on Prevalence, Variety, and Effects." *Archives of Sexual Behavior* 9(3) (1980): 171–94.

Fortune, *M. Sexual Abuse Prevention: A Study for Teenagers.* New York: United Church Press, 1984.

Idem. *Sexual Violence: An Ethical and Pastoral Perspective.* New York: Pilgrim Press, 1983.

Idem. *Sexual Violence: The Unmentionable Sin.* New York: Pilgrim Press, 1983.

Forward, S., and Buck, C. *Betrayal of Innocence: Incest and Its Devastation.* Los Angeles: J. P. Teacher, 1978.

Foster, S., M.D. "Counseling Survivors of Incest." *Medical Aspects of Human Sexuality* (March 1988): 114–24.

Freud, S. The Petiology of Hysteria: *The Complete Psychological Works of Sigmund Freud.* Trans. James Strachey. Standard Edition. London: Hogarth Press (III), 191–221.

Gebhard, P. et al. *Sex Offender: An Analysis of Types.* New York: Harper and Row, 1965.

Gelinas, D. J. "The Persisting Negative Effects of Incest." *Psychiatry* 46 (November 1983): 312–31.

Gelles, R. J., and Cornell, C. P. *Intimate Violence in Families.* Beverly Hills: Sage Publications, 1985.

Gold, E. R. "Long-term Effects of Sexual Victimization in Childhood: An Attributional Approach." *Journal of Consulting and Clinical Psychology* 54(4) (1986): 471–75.

Goodman, B., and Nowak-Scibelli, D. "Group Treatment for Women Incestuously Abused as Children." *International Journal of Group Psychotherapy* 35(4) (October 1985): 531–44.

Goodwin, J. *Sexual Abuse: Incest Victims and Their Families.* Boston: John Wright, 1982.

Gordy, P. L. "Group Work That Supports Adult Victims of Childhood Incest." *Social Casework: The Journal of Contemporary Social Work* (May 1983): 300–07.

Green, A. H. "Self-destructive Behavior in Battered Children." *American Journal of Psychiatry* 85 (October 1978).

Groth, N. *Men Who Rape: The Psychology of the Offender.* New York: Plenum, 1979.

Idem. "The Incest Offender." In *Handbook of Clinical Intervention in Child Sexual Abuse,* edited by Suzanne M. Sgroi. Lexington, MA: Lexington Books, 1983.

Hall, L., and Siobhan, L. *Surviving Child Sexual Abuse: A Handbook for Helping Women Challenge Their Past.* Philadelphia: The Falmer Press, Taylor and Francis, Inc., 1989.

Hartman, M.; Finn, S.; and Leon, G. R. "Sexual-abuse Experiences in a Clinical Population: Comparisons of Familial and Nonfamilial Abuse." *Psychotherapy* 24(2) (Summer 1987): 154–59.

Henderson, D. J. "Incest," in Freedman, A. M.; Kaplan, H. I.; and Sadock, B. J. (eds.). *Comprehensive Textbook of Psychiatry, II.* Baltimore: Williams and Wilkins, 1975.

Idem. "Is Incest Harmful?" *Canadian Journal of Psychiatry* 28 (February 1983): 34–40.

Herman, J. "Recognition and Treatment of Incestuous Families." *International Journal of Family Therapy* 5(2) (Summer 1983):81–91.

Idem. "Father-Daughter Incest." *Signs: Journal of Women in Culture and Society* 2(4) (Summer 1977): 735–56.

Herman, J., and Hirschman, L. "Families at Risk for Father-Daughter Incest." *American Journal of Psychiatry* 138(7) (July 1981): 967–69.

Herman, J.; Russell, D. E. H.; and Trocki, K. "Long-term Effects of Incestuous Abuse in Childhood." *American Journal of Psychiatry* 143(10) (October 1986): 1293–96.

James, J., and Meyerding, J. "Early Sexual Experiences as a Factor in Prostitution." *Archives of Sexual Behavior* 7(1) (1977): 31–42.

Janssen, M. *Silent Scream: I am a Victim of Incest.* Philadelphia: Fortress Press, 1983.

Johnson, S. M. "Integrating Marital and Individual Therapy for Incest Survivors: A Case Study." *Psychotherapy* 26(1) (Spring 1989): 96–103.

Jung, K. G. *Psychology of the Unconscious.* New York: Moffat Yard, 1916.

Kaufman, I.; Peck, A; and Taglori, L. "The Family Constellation and Overt Incestuous Relations Between Father and Daughter." *American Journal of Orthopsychiatry* 24(1954): 266–79.

Kempe, R., and Kempe H. C. *The Common Secret: Sexual Abuse of Children and Adolescents.* New York: Freeman and Company, 1984.

Kinsey, A. C.; Pomeroy, W. B.; and Martin, C. E. *Sexual Behavior in the Human Male*. Philadelphia: Saunders, 1948.

Kinsey, A. C.; Pomeroy, W. B.; Martin, C. E.; et al. *Sexual Behavior in the Human Female*. Philadelphia: Saunders, 1953.

Lindzey, G. "Some Remarks Concerning Incest: The Incest Taboo and Psychoanalytic Theory." *American Psychologist* 40(1967): 1051.

Litin, E.; Giffen, M.; and Johnson, A. "Parental Influence in Unusual Sexual Behavior of Children." *Psychoanalytic Quarterly* 25(1956): 37–55.

Lowenthal, M. F. and Chiriboga, D. "Social Stress and Adaption: Toward a Life-Course Perspective." In D. Eisdorfer and M. P. Lawton (eds.), *The Psychology of Adult Development and Aging*. Washington, D.C.: American Psychological Association, 1973, pp. 281–310.

Lustig, N.; Dresser, J. W.; Spellman, S. W.; and Murray, T. B. "Incest: A Family Group Survival Pattern." *Archives of General Psychiatry* 14 (1966): 31–40.

McCarty, L. M. "Mother-Child Incest: Characteristics of the Offender." *Child Welfare* 65(5) (September/October 1986): 447–58.

McNaron, T., and Morgan, Y., eds. *Voices In the Night: Women Speaking About Incest*. Minneapolis: Cleis Press, 1982.

Malinowsky, B. *Sex and Repression in Savage Society*. London: Routledge and Kegan Paul, 1927.

Maltz, W. "Identifying and Treating the Sexual Repercussions of Incest: A Couples Therapy Approach." *Journal of Sex and Marital Therapy* 14(2) (Summer 1988): 142–52.

Marie, L. *I Must Not Rock*. New York: Daughters Publishing Co., Inc., 1977.

Meiselman, K. *Incest: A Psychological Study of Causes and Effects with Treatment Considerations*. San Francisco: Josey Bass, 1978.

Menaghan, E. G. "Individual Coping Efforts and Family Studies: Conceptual and Methodological Issues." *Marriage and Family Review* 61(1) (1983): 113–35.

Miller, A. *Thou Shalt Not Be Aware: Society's Betrayal of the Child*. Translated by H. and H. Hannum. New York: Farrar, Straus, and Giroux, 1984.

Miller, J. B. *Toward a New Psychology of Women*. Boston: Beacon Press, 1971.

Nelson, J. B. *Embodiment: An Approach to Sexuality and Christian Theology*. Minneapolis: Augsburg Publishing House, 1979.

Nicarthy, G. *Getting Free: A Handbook for the Women In Abusive Relationships*. Seattle: The Seal Press, 1982.

Nicholson, Shirley, ed. *The Goddess Re-awakening*. Wheaton, IL: Theosophical Publishing House, 1989.

Numeroff, R. *A Guide for Health Professionals.* Rockville, MD: Aspen, 1983.

O'Hare, J., and Taylor, K. "The Reality of Incest." *Women and Therapy* 2(2/3) (Summer/Fall 1983): 215–29.

Orr, D. P. "Incest." *American Journal of Disturbed Children* 132 (1978): 1045–53.

Idem. *Adam, Eve, and the Serpent.* New York: Vintage Books, 1988.

Parker, H., and Parker, S. "Father-Daughter Sexual Abuse: An Emerging Perspective." *American Journal of Orthopsychiatry* 56(4) (October 1986): 531–49.

Pellauer, M.; Chester, B.; and Boyajian, J., eds. *Sexual Assault and Abuse: A Handbook for Religious Professionals.* New York: Harper and Row, 1987.

Rascovsky, A., and Rascovsky, M. "On Consummated Incest." *International Journal of Psychoanalysis* 31 (1950): 42–47.

Rist, K. "Incest: Theoretical and Clinical Views." *American Journal of Orthopsychiatry* 49(4) (October 1979): 680–91.

Rosenberg, M. S. "Brief Guide to Office Practice: Adult Behaviors Reflect Childhood Incest." *Medical Aspects of Human Sexuality* (May 1988): 114–24.

Rosenfeld, A. A.; Nadelson, C. C.; and Krieger, M. "Fantasy and Reality in Patients' Reports of Incest." *Journal of Clinical Psychology* 40 (4)(1979): 159–64.

Rush, F. *The Best Kept Secret: Sexual Abuse of Children.* New York: McGraw Hill Book Co., 1980.

Russell, D. E. H. *Sexual Exploitation: Rape, Child Sexual Abuse Workplace Harassment.* Beverly Hills: Sage Publications, 1984.

Idem. *The Secret Trauma: Incest in the Lives of Girls and Women.* New York: Basic Books, Inc., 1986.

Ryan, W. *Blaming the Victim.* New York: Vintage Books, 1976.

Saltman, V., and Solomon, R. S. "Incest and the Multiple Personality." *Psychological Reports* 50 (1982): 1127–41.

Schechner, R. "Incest and Culture: A Reflection On Claude Levi-Strauss." *Psychoanalytic Review* 58(4) (1971–1972): 563–72.

Sgroi, S. *Handbook of Clinical Intervention in Child Sexual Abuse.* Lexington, MA: Lexington Books, 1983.

Shapiro, S. "Self-mutilation and Self-blame in Incest Victims." *American Journal of Psychotherapy* 41(1) (January 1987): 46–54.

Smede, L. B. *Forgive and Forget: Healing the Hurts We Don't Deserve.* New York: Simon and Schuster Inc., 1984.

Stacey, W. A., and Shupe, A. *The Family Secret: Domestic Violence In America.* Boston: Beacon Press, 1983.

Summit, R., and Kryso, J. "Sexual Abuse of Children: A Clinical Spectrum." *American Journal of Orthopsychiatry* 48 (April 1978): 237–51.

Swanson, L., and Biaggio, M. K. "Therapeutic Perspectives on Father–Daughter Incest." *American Journal of Psychiatry* 142(6) (June 1985): 667–74.

Swink, K. K., and Leveille, A. E. "From Victim To Survivor: A New Look at the Issues and Recovery Process for Adult Survivors." *Women and Therapy* 5(2/3) (Summer/Fall 1986): 119–41.

Weinberg, S. K. *Incest Behavior.* New York: Citadel Press, 1955.

Weiner, L. J. "Issues In Sex Therapy With Survivors of Intrafamily Sexual Abuse." *Women and Therapy* 7(2/3) (Summer/Fall 1988): 253–65.

Wells, L. A. "Family Pathology and Father-Daughter Incest: Restricted Psychopathy." *Journal of Clinical Psychiatry* 42(5) (May 1981): 197–202.

Westermarck, E. *History of Human Marriage.* Vol. II. New York: The Allerton Book Company, 1922.

Westermeyer, J. "Incest in Psychiatric Practice: A Description of Patients and Incestuous Relationships." *Journal of Clinical Psychiatry* 39(1978): 643–48.

Resources

C. Henry Kempe National Center for the Prevention & Treatment of Child Abuse and Neglect
1205 Oneida Street
Denver, CO 80220
(303) 321–3963

National Center of Child Abuse and Neglect (NCCAN)
Department of Health and Human Services
P.O. Box 1182
Washington, DC 20013
(202) 245–2856

National Coalition Against Sexual Assault
8787 State Street
East St. Louis, IL 62203
(618) 398–7764

Survivors of Incest International
P.O. Box 21817
Baltimore, MD 21222–6817
(301) 282–3400

VOICES (Victims of Incest Can Emerge Survivors)
in Action, Inc.
P.O. Box 148309
Chicago, IL 60614
(312) 327–1500

National Organization for Victim Assistance
717 D Street, NW
Washington, DC 20004
(202) 232–6682

Incest Survivor Information Exchange
P.O. Box 3399
New Haven, CT 06515

Incest Survivors Anonymous
P.O. Box 5613
Long Beach, CA 90805–0613
(213) 422–1632

Parents United/Sons and Daughters United
(treatment for sexual abuse)
P.O. Box 952
San Jose, CA 95108
(408) 280–5055

Survivors of Physical and Emotional Abuse As Kids (SPEAKS)
c/o Parents Anonymous
7120 Franklin Ave.
Los Angeles, CA 90046
California (800) 352–0386
Outside California (213) 876–0933

Victim Advocacy Network, Inc.
Gail MacDonough, Exec. Dir.
64 Sycamore Rd.
Wayland, MA 01778
    (508) 655–1996